The
Voice
of
Animals

10 Life-Healing Lessons We Can Learn From Animals

Margrit Coates

Matador
9 Priory Business Park,
Wistow Road, Kibworth Beauchamp,
Leicestershire. LE8 0RX
Tel: 0116 279 2299
Email: books@troubador.co.uk
Web: www.troubador.co.uk/matador
Twitter: @matadorbooks

ISBN 978 1788035 262
British Library Cataloguing in Publication Data.
A catalogue record for this book is available from the British Library.

Printed and bound by CPI Group (UK) Ltd, Croydon, CR0 4YY
Typeset in 11pt Minion Pro by Troubador Publishing Ltd, Leicester, UK

Matador is an imprint of Troubador Publishing Ltd

I dedicate this book to all species on this planet.

Praise for this book:

'Every animal has a story to share. Take time to listen and you will learn about kindness, compassion, contentment and the power of the human-animal bond, as this important book reveals.'

Dr Daniel Allen, animal geographer, founder of Pet Nation,
author of *The Nature Magpie*

'Another wonderful, enlightening book from Margrit Coates demonstrating how animals teach us connection in a world so full of separation. Just what we need; fantastic!'

Amanda Newell CHBC, MA Anthrozoology,
Animal-Human relationship consultant

'This book is insightful and thought-provoking; an essential read for anyone wishing to establish a deeper connection with animals. Taking time to stop and "listen" to my patients through the senses establishes an understanding that enables me to advise on all aspects of their care. Acknowledging the needs of animals can enhance our own wisdom and inner peace; this book will help you along that path.'

Sue Devereux BA BVSc MRCVS, equine acupuncturist and chiropractor

'A compelling read providing inspirational stories and tips to help people and animals find a deeper connection. Margrit is an amazing, gentle, yet powerful advocate for animals spreading compassion through this book.'

Suzanne Rogers, IAABC certified equine behaviour consultant,
director of Learning About Animals, co-founder and
programmes advisor at Change For Animals Foundation

'Perfect for everyone who loves animals. The messages are timeless and universal.'

Isabella Allard, Awaken to Brilliance podcast radio

Further Praise for Margrit Coates:

Related to *Connecting with Horses* 'A terrific work and much needed.'

Michael Morpurgo, author of *War Horse*

'In *[Communicating with Animals]*, *Margrit Coates reveals many fascinating and compelling aspects of this little understood "language".'*

Virginia McKenna, OBE, founder trustee of the Born Free Foundation

'*Margrit's gift to animal healing is enormous.*'

Dr Nick Thompson BSc (Vet Sci) Hons,
BVM&S, Vet MFHom, MRCVS, holistic veterinary consultant

'*Margrit Coates creates a sound path for us back to what we have known in our hearts all along.*'

Susan Chernak McElroy, author of *Animals as Teachers and Healers*

Contents

Introduction   xi

1. Let Go   1

2. Listen and Observe   18

3. Open Your Heart   33

4. Be Aware   48

5. Understand   65

6. Shine   77

7. Play   97

8. The Journey is Eternal   112

9. Be a Truth Seeker   125

10. Tune into Healing Energy   137

Useful Information   149

Special Thanks and Credits   154

Introduction

The title of this book, *The Voice of Animals*, has a dual meaning. On one level, my work entails being a 'voice of animals'; however, all animals have a voice of their own as well. Although animals are verbally silent, they offer profound messages through their varied means of communication, expression and even telepathic connection with us.

For many people the world over, animals occupy a hugely important place in their lives. We strive to ensure that those animals in our care are healthy, and worry when they show signs of being unhappy. Perhaps the reason that we are so dedicated to them is because they do so much for us in turn and share our exploration of consciousness. People who love animals understand that the companionship of animals can act as a conduit for improving our own sentience, empathy and self-development.

Animals encourage us to delve into our psyche and to scrutinise our relationships with others, to find a route to inner peace and harmony and a more fulfilling life. They introduce to us possibilities that we may not have previously considered, not least the notion that our emotions and thought processes serve as instructions not only to animals, but to other human beings as well. Animals, and the way that we are with them, hold up a mirror to society itself.

'My life as an animal' was the subject of one of my talks and the concept confused some people at first. It still isn't widely acknowledged by many of us that we humans are animals too, although unlike any other. The reaction to my talk got me thinking about how human-centric our species can be and how much we therefore miss that is relevant to life as a whole. While most of the beings on this planet are nonhuman, their wisdom, experience and insights are often hugely overlooked by humans – to our detriment.

Scientific studies involving animals can add to our knowledge about them, yet all too often such research is flawed, particularly when captive animals are observed. In these instances, data about animal behaviour may be formulated that is not actually typical of the species in its natural habitat; likewise, scientists may often spend time 'discovering' something that people living in close association with animals already know. Science can unfortunately also become a cloak to hide behind, especially when used to deny animal sentience. There is a sector of humanity that dreams only of mechanical or scientific clarity, but such an approach can be blinkered and obscure the rich essence of life. The relationship that animals have with time, for instance, is complex and cannot be studied by mechanical means. To know who animals are, how they think and feel, we need to deploy our consciousness.

Fortunately, there is a group of enlightened and trailblazing scientists today who are taking a different approach and pioneering change as regards the rights of animals, which has resulted in several countries giving animals status as nonhuman persons, and making reforms designed to combat the enormous damage caused to animal wellbeing by factory farming, for instance, which has a knock-on effect on human health too.

As a result of these global campaigns for improvements, ours has become known as the century of the animal. It is as optimists that we embark on such projects and indulge in some species shape-shifting – allowing ourselves to learn a huge amount along the way, as well as to help other species. As animal rights advocate Ricky Gervais has said: 'I believe the greatest privilege in this world is to use your freedom of speech for those who have no voice.' And I wholeheartedly agree with him.

A human-centric bias is unhelpful in terms of our appreciation of this planet, because it leads to fragmentation and much worse: violation of our own peace of mind. We can find ourselves becoming addicted to the toxic energy of consumerism, for instance, and forget the true price we pay when we live in an artificial, soulless world. Our cluttered thinking can become a hindrance to mindfulness and rob us of inner peace.

Learning from animals, and nature, offers the opportunity for spiritual development on a daily basis. I have experienced my fair share of difficulties, experiences that help me empathise with other people, and have discovered through my work as an animal communicator and healer that the secrets of the Universe can be revealed through our connection to animals, affording us enchanting experiences when we learn to look, listen and feel beyond the limitations and boundaries of the material world. The collective traits and characteristics of other species can act as pointers to life lessons. Every animal, bird, sea creature, and insect has the experiences of its own life to share with us, as well as possessing knowledge of the evolution of the species to which it belongs. Through this fascinating bundle of collective communication, we are invited to contemplate what we can learn from animals. In doing so, we will find we expand the scope of our attention and acquire a deeper understanding of the intimacy of language that is not confined to verbal or written words alone.

All species communicate; it is not just a human attribute. And by 'communicate' I mean through an energy process that involves a telepathic level of awareness, as suggested earlier. We see examples of this kind of awareness all around us, every day. For instance, countless times my cats will suddenly get up in unison and move to another part of the house or garden. There is no shout of '*Hey guys, let's all go to the blue sofa in the other room now*', but somehow a message to perform an activity is exchanged.

Similarly, I often care for a group of dogs who are adept at reading minds or intention. When I'm looking after them, I might be reading a book and think to myself that perhaps I would like another walk on the beach before lunch, and the dogs will suddenly appear by my side whining, barking and wagging tails. Yet whenever I leave them to set out on a longer trip away, they know the difference between that and a normal excursion. On those occasions, the dogs don't race me to the door in the expectation that I might be taking them somewhere; instead they sit with morose faces, not even coming near me.

How do they know such things? The reason, put simply, is because our minds transmit messages and the energy of everything overlaps. In this way, the awareness, thoughts and feelings of other beings are constantly in contact with us – whether we realise this or not. On a subconscious level, of course, we are fully aware each moment of this phenomenon taking place. By learning to utilise our own intuitive processes, we can aspire to step into other worlds intentionally. When we discover how to blend our conscious mind with the invisible subconscious, this is where the mysterious true nature of animals will be revealed to us, as well as the lessons that can be learnt from them. It can be an exhilarating, life-enhancing experience – as the stories in the book reveal.

Every animal that I have met, and there have been many tens of thousands, teaches me to stand back from our human, earthbound mode and see way beyond it to realms that at one time I might once have considered impossible to reach. Wherever I come across animals, their truthful essence attracts me like a light in the darkness of human-created chaos. They are powerful teachers, waiting for us to respond to the lessons they have to offer. This is why, wherever I find myself, I take the time to notice the living beings around me, and acknowledge our interconnected nature by greeting them: '*Hello, how are you?*' This communication often results in an energy exchange taking place, which in turn triggers a processing of new knowledge on my part.

With the help of animals, I have experienced a multitude of lessons about 'being'. Every animal I have met has taken me on an incredible journey of learning, communication and healing. Animals have a voice, albeit sometimes silent, and part of my dedication to them involves acting as the voice for the voiceless. It is astounding how much I am learning about life, loss, love, relationships, communication, healing and myself along the way.

As the world appears to become increasingly troubled and chaotic, spirituality can help to counterbalance the effects of this and find a path forward. Spirituality is an ever-evolving process, and because Universal knowledge is infinite we are naturally unable to take it in all at once. This is where animals can help us out, by adding to our understanding gradually, one step at a time, through their ongoing presence in our lives – although sometimes this can happen in a spectacular way, as the stories in this book will show.

All animals have a story to tell: everything is of equal importance and their stories stack together as a whole. It's been said that some people come into our lives as blessings, others as lessons. Animals bring both attributes, to help us as life-healing guides. Each chapter in this book focuses on a particular lesson they offer us, while the book as a whole offers insights on all of life.

Through connecting with the inner voice of the animals, we are afforded an opportunity to investigate our own natures as living, thinking and feeling beings. Life is so hectic these days that many of us seek new ways to find harmony – and what could be a better or easier route to peace than by listening to a much-loved dog, cat or horse, or by connecting with other animals? Through our interactions with animals, we are invited to become more observant, better listeners, to increase our patience, awareness and wisdom and become more contented within ourselves. Through engaging more fully with the whole of life, we become advocates for the rights and protection of all beings, both human and nonhuman, thus adding that vitally important 'e' to human – becoming humane in the fullest sense.

So, I'd like to give a big Thank You to the animals – with your help I have discovered who I am. With your ongoing guidance I am gaining further knowledge, understanding and insights. You are the most wonderful teachers!

Here, in this book, is what I've learnt …

Margrit Coates

1. Let Go

Did I waste time, allowing my mind to blot out consciousness of my connection with the world around me? Or was I present in the moment, at one with all life, thereby allowing myself to evolve into a more enlightened human being? As a student of animal teachings, that is something I ask myself at the end of each day.

Like other people, I have days when I can't seem to focus. On this particular day, I was trying to write but inspiration was proving elusive and my mind seemed as blank as the sheet of paper on the desk in front of me. Then there was a knock on the door and in came Oscar, followed by his human companions, John and Eve. As soon as I looked into those amber-coloured eyes, I felt a familiar frisson of anticipation and knew that an animal teacher had arrived to sort me out.

From an early age, Belgian shepherd dog Oscar had demonstrated his strength of character. The family who had originally taken him as a puppy had found him to be too wilful and boisterous for them to train. So six months later Oscar had been sent back to the breeder, who then placed the youngster with John and Eve. The couple weren't daunted by Oscar's strong opinions, which they laughingly described as his resilience. Instead, they developed an immediate, strong bond with the dog, who thrived under their care and attention.

Oscar was now eleven years old, and, although he was still mentally sharp, he had developed a serious heart condition. With the blessing of their vet, John and Eve were exploring holistic ways to help him enjoy a good quality of life. With his typically feisty attitude, Oscar still romped along on walks and played with hectic abandon, albeit suffering from increasing bouts of fatigue.

Today, Oscar's eyes scanned me for visual information, but – more than that – I knew he was sensing who I was as a being. Bounding forward, he ran around me several times before coming to sit by my side, which the couple declared was a sure sign the dog liked me. It was a pleasing start, and Oscar's zest for life was evident as he followed me around while I put on a CD of relaxing music and made some tea.

During the healing therapy session that followed, I sensed Oscar communicate to me that the couple needed guidance about their own state of mind. Taken aback, I stopped myself from glancing in their direction, wondering what this was all about. My work as a healer has taught me that animals communicate with each other through an unseen energy system, and that we humans also have the ability to tune into this energy and sense what animals are saying. Animals are particularly sensitive to people's thoughts and moods, and I learnt from Oscar that he was becoming increasingly anxious about the couple's tendency to dwell on aspects of his condition. In fact, so much so, that I sensed Oscar was thoroughly fed up with it. To highlight this fact, the dog sighed, and, resting his head on a paw, left me to raise the topic with them.

I completely understood the couple's concern about Oscar's health and how much they were worried about him. When life throws a curve ball at us, it's easy to become consumed by the situation, not least because there is often a lot for us to consider and organise. Both John and Eve admitted to having become immersed in Oscar's health issues to the extent that they thought and talked about little else. Whatever they did together, they focused on the negative aspects of Oscar's life – including his past as well as his future possibilities, a tendency I'd noticed earlier during the consultation. Even when eating their dinner, they would look over at Oscar and make comments such as, 'Oh what a shame, that poor dog!' And, when tucking Oscar up in his bed at night, they'd wonder if the dog would still be alive in the morning; unbeknown to them, this was the lasting thought of the day that they left with Oscar.

John then explained that nowadays he became sad at the mere thought of taking Oscar on outings because they might not have much time left together. Suddenly, Oscar sprang up from his relaxed state, barked furiously and promptly left the room to go outside.

Unfolding before me was a clear and profound lesson from a very clever dog. Oscar was issuing an ultimatum to the humans in his life to stop clinging to their counterproductive ideas and thoughts. 'Can you see what is going on here?' I asked. 'Oscar is showing you how your constant focus on problems distresses him. It's not helpful for either you or him.'

John and Eve admitted to being shocked at the power of their thought energy and how animals might react to it. Their lack of self-awareness and negative attitude – albeit unintentional, because the couple loved their dog more than anything else – had broken the spell of the healing peace that Oscar experienced earlier during the session, and this was why the dog now wanted to distance himself from us. We had been shown quite clearly that Oscar was frustrated, disappointed and annoyed with their doom-and-gloom attitude, which was out of synch with the dog's own desire to focus on a positive moment. We were being reminded that, through their chaotic thoughts, humans can sabotage both their own and an animal's peace and calm.

As well as having an adverse effect in our own lives, including our relationships with others, negative thinking is disempowering for all beings. The complex way that the human mind and psyche work has a knock-on effect on the wellbeing of any animals that we associate with. Studies show that animals will try to move away from people with destructive thoughts, as Oscar had so aptly demonstrated. Such destructive thoughts and lapses in our awareness are often caused by fear, envy or dissatisfaction. Out of these springs a desire for things to be other than they are, rather than accepting what is real. We could all do with practising a little self-reflection from time to time, encouraging ourselves to grow stronger as individuals and overcome obstacles. If we are lucky, sometimes someone comes along who challenges how we view the world and our role in it – and that 'someone' can be an animal companion.

I have long been encouraged by the example of animals not to become defined by my problems, something which helped me greatly when I was seriously ill with breast cancer a few years ago. I did not want to find myself swept up in a situation in which people were talking about me as if I were a victim. At the time, it felt right for me to ask people not to talk about my illness in my presence but to send me their positive thoughts instead, thereby affording me the clear head space I needed to fight my illness and overcome it.

In order to free our minds from a whirlpool of despair and negative opinions, we need to make a conscious decision to change our way of thinking; and fortunately John and Eve readily agreed to try to do this. All the same, it took a little while for Oscar to return from the courtyard and settle with us again. After explaining to him that the humans in his life had promised to modify their behaviour, Oscar flopped down by my side, and these words were revealed into my consciousness:

> Let go! Stop wasting time in the past, it has gone. The future doesn't have any meaning because it's not here. This moment is real and we need to enjoy it. Life consists of precious present moments, and it is motivating to move along in that timeframe. In the here and now, I am neither young nor old, I just am. Join me in the moment and we can spontaneously enjoy life together.

Animals have a sense of awareness which, rather than being superficial, concerns the whole self. They seek to look on the bright side of life, instead of wondering 'why am I like this?' The ability to find completeness in the moment will enable us to experience satisfaction in our own lives, and help us to develop the courage we need to deal with whatever the future might throw at us.

4

Having gone home equipped with tips about how best to accommodate Oscar's wishes, including briefing their family and friends not to raise the topic of the dog's ill health, the couple returned a week later with the news that changing their mindset had helped them become happier with life in general. As a result they were no longer afraid of what the future might bring. Oscar looked up when they mentioned this, then rolled over onto his side and fell into a deep sleep almost instantly. Teaching humans was obviously a tiring business.

Paying attention

Whenever I find myself drifting off into unnecessary levels of worry, my salvation comes from being with animals and appreciating their simple yet profound approach to being alive. This isn't to say that we shouldn't delve into the memories that we hold, recalling events and experiences, or plan for the future. We can lose our way, though, if we continue to fret about the past and forage into 'what if' scenarios concerning the future, with the result that we stumble through the present, completely overlooking the possibility of enjoying positive experiences here and now. When we relax into the present we will find ourselves harmonising with the moment. The truth is that we only really exist in the present moment anyway, so we might as well pay attention to it.

I have read that our entire existence is experienced through the mind. Yet through my connection to animals I know this is not strictly true. Animals have not lost the ability to tune into the intuitive sixth sense – our soul voice, which humans have largely come to ignore. The mind runs parallel with that centre, and, like animals do, we can pay attention to it for the benefit of not just our mind but our experience of life as a whole. By setting ourselves free to observe each moment as it unfolds, we can appreciate that the gateway to a fulfilling spiritual life resides in our soul.

The whole

Having been 'owned' by cats for decades, I know that they too have a natural ability to live in the moment, and are able to radiate that power to help us over life's stumbling blocks. A cat's mastery of the art of focusing is a vivid reminder of the value of being mindful in each and every second that passes.

Pinned to the wall above my desk is an insight I gleaned many years ago from a soul-mate cat, Casey. One evening, I was particularly worried about a difficult work project and concerned about how I was going to sort it out. Casey came to the rescue; as he stretched out on my lap I heard his voice transmit these wise words: '*Release the trivia and you can see everything you need to.*' Whilst playing with my cat and cuddling him, I found that the disruptive energy of my unwanted thoughts had simply dispersed. The next morning I woke up with a solution to the problem clear in my mind, and best of all I had a feeling of relaxed anticipation about the day ahead.

Animals, it seems, are connected to a core of complete knowledge, which they wish to share with us. For our part, we need to be accepting so that we are able to hear them. It is not just the mind that benefits through our paying attention; all of our senses can serve us with greater significance, because they become accented and magnified whenever we decide to focus and tune into the living world around us.

Slow down and resonate

As the animals in our lives say to us: '*Have an open mind because it can raise your consciousness.*' Indeed, the alternative – a closed mind – can allow negativity to fester, resulting in a state whereby our mind is so crammed full of thoughts, it prevents us from being rational. Our focus is then distracted from the whole, with the result that we become fragmented ourselves and less clearly defined as individuals. This in turn prevents us from appreciating the wisdom of other life forms as we explore our human journey. Interaction with animals can help us appreciate the difference between the chatter of our minds, which bombards us with constant information, and our lucid soul voice, which resonates on the same wavelength as that of all other beings. Through this soul connection, we belong to a complex nucleus of billions of lives.

Because they are highly sensitive to our moods, animals are a good barometer of the effect that our own state of mind has on others. Animals engage with us as energy beings, including those times when we allow our mind to run away with jostling thoughts and send out mixed messages. We can lose our way by placing too much emphasis on even the smallest difficulty instead of reflecting on happy moments. By virtue of their very nature and their focus on life in the moment, animals encourage us to put an end to our negative thought processes before they grow into something that adversely impacts our lives. The minds of animals are more orderly and don't succumb to the intricate mental and emotional games that we do; yet even so animals possess a powerful presence. Animal friends help us to combat stress by encouraging us to take our time to act calmly and combat endless distractions. They are an example of how to 'be', rather than just be constantly 'doing'.

It can seem impossible to free ourselves from the distraction of a rampantly chattering mind, though. Thankfully animals are there to help us and offer valuable life lessons to guide us through the maze of day-to-day challenges. The foundation of their lessons as a whole is grounded in the importance of letting go and surrendering to each moment, which then allows us to note elements of time as they occur and shift. As Oscar had demonstrated that day, animals remind us of the need to give ourselves permission to put aside everyday concerns and distractions, including scrambled thoughts that spin around in our heads like a never-ending circle. By freeing ourselves from external influences we can slow down and sense the unfettered peace of our soul.

Several decades ago, science confirmed that our thoughts can affect our moods and emotions. Following on from that understanding, it became apparent that the reverse holds true – our inner worlds influence our thoughts and consciousness. A person might, for instance, look at a dull grey sky and feel gloomy about it due to a perception of what it signifies and whether or not he or she finds it pleasing. Whereas an animal will perceive the greyness and accept it as relevant to the weather, season or time of day, knowing that it is what it is. If we were to be like the birds, when we take in the vista of the sky we would resonate with a level of consciousness that reminds us that it is not just grey, but full of information, texture and shades of colour.

Nurturing this kind of development of the mind helps the soul to flourish and will ultimately provide a foundation of health and happiness to last a lifetime. There is no better time to start engaging with the world in this way than when young, and encouraging children to learn from animal wisdom will not only help them to maintain a healthy mental outlook, but also sow the seeds of an interest in all life forms as worthy teachers.

Switch off to tune in

We miss so much that is important through commotion and activity. Modern life has become cacophonous and as such plays an adverse role in terms of our being able to keep a clear and focused mind. If we seek to heal our lives then our phones, tablets, laptops and computers need to be switched off for part of each day – these objects are devoid of emotional intelligence, spiritual memory or nurturing capacity. We need mental space if we are to develop spiritually and open a channel that will allow us to tune into the multitude of creatures around us. In this hectic century, we have lost the ability to gather sensory information, and have instead replaced that skill with an aptitude for sifting through the data provided by technology, whose usage has become addictive.

> In order to articulate through our intuition, we need to create 'time out' from distractions. This allows us to be in synch with the resonance of the planet.

I've made it a habit never to have anything electrical or related to technology in the bedroom in order to limit my exposure to unhealthy distractions. Over-reliance on gadgets has resulted in our losing the ability to feel comfortable in our own company, and prevents us from sensing the nuances of our innate, inner wisdom. Animals, however, are not subject to this kind of interruption of their awareness and this is why they remain examples of a pure, unfettered connection to the cosmos, helping us find respite even if we have difficulties to face.

Animal teachers are everywhere

We don't only learn from encounters with companion animals – as the following incident reminded me.

My day had started in a fairly routine way. Shower, feed the animals, breakfast, walk round the garden, check emails. A message pinged in from someone whose demands were taking an unreasonable amount of time to deal with. The news on the radio was full of political disarray, squabbling and financial crisis; a neighbour was using noisy machinery close to my office window; finally, I managed to smear chocolate down my new white shirt and the printer ran out of ink. That was the tipping point for my day; by now my thoughts were completely disorganised. As I tried in vain to read, the words danced around on the page senselessly.

And then I found the mouse.

Stepping into the garden in the hope of finding some inner calm, I noticed a field mouse shivering by the stem of a rose tree. When I stooped down to take a closer look he did not run away; his bead-like eyes stared up at me with what seemed like a plea for help. Gently, I scooped him into my hands and went to sit on the garden bench. On closer inspection the mouse seemed to have an injured leg so I automatically went into healing mode, cupping my hands over his soft brown body and feeling the familiar heat of beneficial energy manifest itself.

I kept peeping through my fingers to see what the mouse was doing, but he just sat there looking at me whenever I uncovered his face. Talking to the mouse, I asked questions about the nature of the injury and whether there was pain. The heat under my hands intensified – experience has taught me that the size of an animal bears no relation to the strength of their energy field. This tiny mouse had a huge vibrating resonance, and I found myself listening to that energy and thinking about what I could learn from it.

Several times I put the mouse down onto the ground, but he struggled to walk so I took him back onto my lap for more healing help. After a while I carried him to a bird bath and dribbled a drop of water around his mouth; it touched me when he opened his mouth and drank in the water. I had been right – he was thirsty. As always occurs in such situations, I found my mind gathering information as it unfolded: the shape of head, ears, nose, fur texture and the gentle acceptance of my presence. An hour had gone by since the mouse and I had become acquainted, and I found that I was enjoying myself immensely. The disturbance within me was oozing away to leave space for stillness to enter in its place. Life had gone from feeling irritating to being quite beautiful. Time spent with animals teaches us that when we let go, a small change can have a big effect.

I was expecting a phone call so before I returned to my office I wandered into the garage with my precious friend safe in my hands, and found what I was looking for – a box pierced with small holes that I keep for injured birds and small creatures to recuperate in. I carefully placed the mouse inside with food and water. When I checked on the mouse later he was climbing over twigs in the box. Perhaps it was fanciful thinking on my part, but he seemed pleased to see me.

Back we went to the garden seat, the mouse again on my lap. I told him that he was beautiful and that I loved him – and I truly meant it. I had a yearning admiration too for his ability to live without the distracting trivia that can spoil a human day. During my reverie and focus on the mouse, I became aware of a moment naturally evolving – when the past and future took their leave, and I drifted along in the present, blending with seemingly endless waves of quietude. Only that moment existed; it was constant, endless and profound. Time had no meaning as I sensed the mouse join me in the powerful peace of the now.

> Animals help us realise that our time is made up of moments in which we can discover revealing insights about the important things in life.

I placed the mouse down onto the grass and, clearly feeling better, he moved off out of sight underneath some dense shrubbery. Instantly, I missed him and I poked around in the undergrowth but he was gone. The profound simplicity of our shared time together had helped me find stillness and 'the moment'. I had been reminded how easy it was to achieve this state with animal guidance, no matter what the species. Later that day I kissed a cat, cuddled a dog and wound my arms around the neck of a horse. My contentment was now luxuriously deep.

It was a precious experience for me: two seemingly very different souls sharing an experience of oneness. There are millions of animal helpers waiting for humans to awaken to the consciousness of life on Earth, and each and every day I invite those teachers into my life.

Let go of an agenda, and set your intention

Another block to awareness can occur when we ignore the promptings of our soul voice and instead become controlled by an agenda. Humans are fond of agendas, which are often self-serving and ego-driven. When we are in thrall to an agenda, we are subconsciously anticipating an outcome that we desire, or need approval for, rather than allowing events to unfold naturally. In this way we set ourselves up to become disappointed or frustrated. This type of behaviour creates a block to our letting go and connecting with the moment, as well as being something that repels interest from animals.

Control is an element of any agenda and stress can arise through our trying to micro-manage every aspect of our lives, including our relationships with animals. If we have an agenda, it can, for instance, be tempting to project our wishes onto whatever an animal's problems seem to be, instead of considering the situation from the animal's viewpoint. When asked to communicate with an animal with the purpose of giving instructions to make it behave in a way that suits the human in the equation, I point out that ultimately we ourselves are responsible for controlling our thoughts, responses and actions – and it is this inner world that animals respond to.

In contrast, our intuition thrives when we allow ourselves to go into the neutral zone of being in the now, which enables us to pick up on the information that the animals wish to pass on to us – and which also allows us to realise our intentions in relation to them and our own lives. I appreciate that there might be some confusion about the difference between the definition of intention and agenda. The way I view it, intention can be conscious or subconscious, and it relates to our desire for life to unfold in a certain way. But unlike a fixed agenda, which creates a stumbling block, once we set an intention we can leave it in the ether and see how it manifests.

The more that I pay attention to the voice of animals, the more I find that my intentions come to fruition – even though this might not be in quite the way I had originally imagined, as the Universe reacts in its wisdom. It might take a long time for the Universe to respond, but intention can't be forced or coerced into action – otherwise it becomes an agenda! Animals encourage us to live at a frequency of intention and open-minded generosity, as this next story shows …

An encounter with a foal

The pretty foal stood by the side of the road, relaxing in the afternoon spring sunshine, occasionally flicking his little tail to swat away a fly. Tufts of brown hair stuck up in the air between his ears, his gangly legs balanced on tiny hooves. On seeing him, I stopped to enjoy the spectacle, as did other drivers passing through the New Forest National Park, where ponies, donkeys, sheep, cattle and pigs roam freely. The foal's mother grazed nearby with other mares, and I noticed how she watched her baby even though she was eating, a mother's protective instincts alert for danger.

One by one, people tried to approach the foal, either to touch him or to take photos, and then he would move away to step behind his mother where he felt safer. It was clear that he didn't want the alien species to get too close to him. Sitting on the grass far enough away from the herd not to bother them, I watched the scene and understood a little more about human and animal behaviour.

Another car stopped by the side of the road and a man and young boy got out – father and son I assumed – and took a few steps away from their vehicle towards the group of ponies. There was a look of rapture on the boy's face, which grabbed my attention; he was staring as though seeing something wonderful and amazing for the first time in his life. The boy knelt down and remained motionless, the foal turning to watch him, a connection forming. The foal took a few faltering steps, then skipped along to stand before the boy. They viewed each other; it seemed like neither of them knew how to proceed or what was required of them.

> Animals are an integral part of our evolution as a species. Whilst many humans have lost the art of being guided by intuition, animals remain sensitive to energy and act accordingly. If we are carrying with us anything other than calm, respectful energy they are disturbed by it.
>
> We need to be mindful of our non-verbal cues and avoid assaulting animals with our disruptive stress. Taking a thoughtful approach in every aspect of our lives not only makes for better relationships with other humans but also relieves us of our mental burdens.

Tentatively the boy held out his hand and rested it on the foal's neck – and that is how they remained together for several minutes.

Walking over to the boy's father, I asked if he might like me to take a photo as he didn't appear to have a camera with him. The man explained that they were passing through the area. Coming from a large industrial city, his seven-year-old son had had no previous contact with horses.

'My son's often talked about wanting to meet a horse,' explained the man. 'When we noticed the foal he shouted at me to stop the car. He became so emotional that I honestly thought he was going to burst into tears.'

The foal's interest in the boy now made even more sense to me. The boy didn't want to take anything from him or make anything happen, or put on a show. He just wanted to experience the foal in an act of being. The foal, young as he was, sensed the difference between people wanting to grab him, and the energy of a human who was there with acceptance. Whatever would come to pass that was instigated by the foal was going to be OK with the boy. If all that he had taken home with him had been the memory of seeing the little horse that would have been enough. Instead a dream had come true and I was able to send him a photo of that moment.

Boy and foal: a magical moment

Breathe

Luna, a thoroughbred mare, confirmed for me the importance of freeing ourselves of stress and tension. Jody, the horse's carer, seemed uptight and was quick to tell me that she didn't feel close to Luna, who appeared friendly and placid. Jody blamed herself for having done things wrong and missing what her horse was communicating. I explained that life can be difficult for humans, because we often look in the wrong places for wisdom or follow bad advice instead of using our intuition to tune into animals – and while I spoke, Luna stood there nodding her head. The horse nodded again when I suggested that Jody should join me in a few minutes of meditative breathing, as I thought this would help her relax.

When I sat down on a stool later on to make notes about the session, Luna came up to me with her head sideways and hanging low, her right eye almost touching my face. The energy radiating from Luna's eye into mine was mesmerising and I felt humbled to be in her master teacher presence. A huge amount of information can seep into to us in one glance from an animal, and while we may not even know what it is at the time, it often surfaces when we most need it. Luna touched my notebook with her nose, before dribbling some half-chewed hay onto the spot where I had just jotted down an insight gained during my conversation with her:

Letting go is the first step of awakening. Remember to breathe through problems so that you can think clearly.

I softly stroked Luna's face, her eyelid lowering briefly like a knowing wink. Turning, she moved away and I was left with her blessing.

Whenever we feel stressed, anxious, fearful or angry, these disruptive emotions set us on the way to formulating more of the same. The world that we create inside our head can cause us more problems than the world around us.

An animal's behaviour is often a reflection of human mental activity. As Luna did when she touched my notebook, animals often communicate that due to stress and mental activity, people have a tendency to hold their breath or breathe in a shallow way. This creates physical tension, blocks clear thinking and prevents us from paying attention. '*Please tell my person to relax and breathe properly*' is something that I often hear animals communicate.

How to let go – Illuminated Breathing

A common question that people put to me is, 'How can I "let go" and be in the moment?' They also ask, 'How can I cut loose from overwhelming distracting trivia and instead appreciate wholeness right now?'

Our breath can hold the key to calm, and it's a good idea to do a daily breathing exercise, even for just a few minutes. With minimal practice and in hardly any time, we can learn to regulate our thinking through the breath. Because animals pay attention to our breathing, when we relax this helps them detach from our anxieties and respond more favourably to us.

Try this:
- Switch off technological devices – although you may find it helpful to play meditation music at a low volume to help create a relaxing ambience.
- Sit or lie comfortably. Take in a deep breath and, as you do so, imagine drawing in positive energy. On the out-breath slightly open your mouth and blow, purposefully calming your energetic field as you do so. Do this six times.
- Now breathe in slowly for a count of five seconds, then breathe out for a count of six seconds. Do this for a minute. This technique is known to alter brain chemistry, acting in a similar way to anti-anxiety medication.
- Feel the ebb and flow of your breath moving throughout your whole body, revitalising your energy.

One of the energy states in a body is light. Its strength increases when we are calm, illuminating our energy field. Mastering focused breathing helps us to achieve this state, which is why I call it 'Illuminated Breathing'.

Breathe more...

The Illuminated Breathing exercise can be taken to a deeper level.
- Raise your arms to waist height with your hands facing each other.
- As you breathe deeply and evenly, tune in with your hands to the rhythm of the breath energy that flows within your body. Sense it

expand and contract between your hands like a tide ebbing and flowing on a beach.

- Now project your mind upwards, into the sky, as you keep following the in and out of the rhythm of your breath. A new energy will slowly and subtly start to move your hands, inwards and outwards like you are playing a squeezebox. You are now sensing the resonance of the energy breath of the Universe. You notice that both energies – your breathing rate and the Universal breath – synchronise.
- Instead of moving backwards and forwards, the flow of energy starts to stack into a kind of spiral, but without a top or bottom, and no beginning or end. Your inner perception broadens and you find that you are in the midst of a long continuous wave of 'this moment'. You may now find yourself taking several deep breaths and tension releasing in your body.

At first, the focus required in this exercise may be a little difficult to maintain, but with practice it can become so easy that you will be able to engage quickly, dipping in and out of the mental expansion at will. Your mind goes into what I call a freewheeling 'neutral state'. As if by magic, a feeling of relaxation ensues.

You can also repeat the exercise by sitting with an animal and sensing their breathing, noticing how your energies blend together. This act often triggers us into being able to sense silent communication from animals. It is a good idea to get into the habit of practising a breathing exercise when you're with animals at any time, to help strengthen your connection with them. When we let go, breathe evenly and deeply and enjoy the moment, we have the best chance of hearing the voice of animals.

Over the years, I've travelled far and wide to this and that seminar, where various human teachers have extolled the virtues of 'letting go to be in the moment', yet at first I never really got to grips with the concept. Then one day it dawned on me that the solution was there, right by my side – the real teachers of this skill were animals. And I have never looked back. As we have seen, animals, through their clever and sensible attentiveness, encapsulate the ability to live in the present moment, which is one reason why I seek out their company and learn a little bit more from them at each and every opportunity. I am always left with the feeling that there is so much more to discover, as well as a sense of wonder that animals have such a complex depth of awareness.

Inattentive and Insensitive   **or**   Attentive and Sensitive

Through the company of animals we are encouraged to move away from a cluttered mindset and approach each day with a positive attitude. When we are in a neutral mental state, the chains of our intellect and fixed thinking are loosened. This means that we are better able to move mentally towards the direction of guidance. Animals prefer to be with us when we are free from a fixed agenda and fluid in our approach to paying attention.

2. Listen and Observe

When we tune into animals, we are invited to move away from illusion and from our seemingly insatiable need to focus on superficial imagery. Instead, we find we can clearly see an infinite existence.

Let me share a recent memory with you: I am strolling to a bench with a dog. As we walk, we play and hug, the dog licking and nibbling at my fingers, tail wagging with joy at the attention I am giving him. When we reach our destination, he flops down by my side, and now we are both looking around at the landscape. The previous day we'd come to this very same seat, tucked away on a dirt footpath at the edge of a shrub-covered slope overlooking the sea. The view here is stunning, with much to admire – but the day before I'd left this spot feeling that I had missed much of importance because I'd been accompanied on my walk by a group of humans.

While it was of course good to catch up with friends, our chatter was often noisy and eventually became intrusive. Whenever something caught my eye, such as a flock of geese flying low over the sea, the sun playing hide and seek with the clouds, or the breeze pulling at a fern frond and dipping it like a pecking bird into a rock pool, there was no time to inspect these things, and my thoughts weren't free to meander and add to my knowledge of the Universe. Although I'd registered the possibilities of this place as special in terms of recharging my batteries, I had gone home feeling strangely empty.

Today, as I sit on the bench, I sense how much more at ease I am as a result of the conversation between the dog, Benny, and myself being unspoken, yet full of empathic perception. Benny does not intrude into my thoughts; therefore I am able to listen and simultaneously observe the environment, perceiving its relevance to what I need to learn in life. Now I have time to study the weather and the shape of the clouds, which reflect flickering shards of light downwards to bounce and twist off the rippling waves. I have long mused over the way Nature moves her elements around as if they are being constantly observed, with a prevailing underlying sense that they *should* be noticed by all creatures, and especially us.

All around me, tucked under bushes and within clumps of grass, flowers quiver in the breeze along the shore line. A loud squawk nearby makes me jump and I notice a seagull landing on a wall, hooked beak gaping open and head tilted back as though looking up at something I can't see. Maybe it is a salute to his friends high above the drifting clouds, so I listen harder to the bird's call, knowing that it must be projecting a message to other gulls. I try to intercept the conversation and notice how my senses are striving to make me a more integrated and interactive member of the Universe. It feels important to observe myself as part of this system and to be aware of my role within it.

Then Benny decides to exhibit his effortless sensory skills, his nose pointing downwards, twitching, and his ears pricked. Following Benny's gaze, I notice a young rabbit hopping in and out of the shrubs scattered along the ridge of the slope. Benny gets to his feet, wagging his tail slightly, and more rabbits pop up, until a whole family is darting about, skipping and leaping because they have the freedom to do so. I focus on their shapes, on their differences in size, colour and movements. The seagull rises into the air, squawking as he flies low over our heads, white wings waving a goodbye, and the rabbits vanish down into their underground homes.

Nothing is insignificant or trivial; I recall how, as I sat on the beach that day, all around me were layers upon layers of multidimensional visual information, scents, sounds and rhythms. It felt good to be there as a witness of life in that place, in that moment. Time did not move me about for a while, and therefore I didn't have any urge to think … just to feel.

Benny sat down again by my side, still scenting the air, so I closed my eyes to try to pick up what he could smell wafting around – and detected a faint fishy aroma, followed by the scent of pine and crushed grass. The focus required meant my hearing also became more acute and I found myself listening to the sound of the breeze, noticing how it undulated in tone like an energetic voice. It dawned on me that animals tune into sounds like this for information much as we might listen to a radio-station news bulletin. The air seemed untrammelled by manmade noise, but I was listening so intently that I heard many sounds in the silence. I was getting the hang of how to do this now.

Opening my eyes again, I looked down at Benny. He was intently staring to the left, towards rocks at the water's edge – but I saw nothing. I knew, though, that something must be there, and sure enough the prow of a kayak poked around the rocks, followed by another boat, both propelled by yellow-attired paddlers. Marvelling at how, despite the sound of waves slapping against the rocks, Benny had been able to know the boats were there before they'd come into view, made me realise how stunted my own senses were. Benny turned his attention to other things and for half an hour or so I listened and looked around, guided by whatever interested him. My contemplation became a powerful lesson, and I realised that many of the answers to our concerns in life lie in listening to the magnificence of our planet, rather than paying attention to the bigotries of the human species. It made so much sense that suddenly I felt thoroughly peaceful.

Benny bumped my knee with his nose and then my pocket, asking for his blue squidgy ball. Returning to the track behind us, we continued our walk, with me rolling the ball for Benny to chase. As we moved along I made sure to keep scanning everything about me so I could progress with my learning.

Animals teach us that we can miss many important pieces of information by not paying attention with our soul. As the world becomes ever more troubled due to political and social unrest, people are increasingly recognising the help that animals offer us. Through the potential guidance of animals we can find inner peace – the best medicine that there is to help us enjoy life.

Place of peace

Deep inside us is a place that is super quiet. The quality of this stillness is beyond compare, and, in order to experience it, we need to possess a willingness to be quiet ourselves. To find stillness means letting go of negative influences, and we can achieve this by opening an inspired space within ourselves that allows for the expansion of our soul. This space then becomes a gateway to contentment and harmony, and through it we can even access the core of Universal knowledge.

Animals can help us access this gateway. There is a form of advanced intelligence within each of us that listening to animals can activate, which can help lead us away from hatred and envy to a place of positive, intelligent living. Humans are only just scratching the surface of our awareness, because, as a species, listening and observing soul to soul has not been high on our agenda. This is why a manifestation of permanent harmony and coherence has not yet appeared in our world. However, this sense of unity is something that I have often felt when with animals – sensing their desire for harmony within us, not from the perspective of benefiting their own egos, but because it matters for our own personal development and self-respect.

> In order to experience contentment and harmony we need to open a space within us that allows for soul expansion. To experience stillness, it is very important to possess a willingness to be quiet. This is our gateway to a place of inner peace.

Animals remind us that 'listening' is a spectrum. It is not just about receiving information with our ears; it involves using all the senses in order to grasp completely all the key information that can help us in various situations. Listening forms part of the gateway to that inner stillness I mentioned, and we can enter it by stepping back a little from human influences so that we can hear the unseen and notice the invisible.

Animals taught me long ago to see the world through a new perspective. I learned from them the value of communicating via the intuition and sixth sense; the importance of listening rather than talking; and that we need to have conversations with them as part of a two-way process. Listening through the vital sixth sense is something we can all do, and it often occurs before we realise what is happening. The quieter we become the more we can hear.

Animals constantly hear us, because they listen to our soul voice, which is a blueprint of who we are. Theirs is a high level of awareness that we humans need to aspire to, so that we don't chase trivia and miss the significant things in life. They invite us to sharpen our senses so that we observe what is really there, rather than attempting to impose our will and presence on situations, which is a recipe for potential chaos and confusion.

If we follow the example of animals and learn to listen and practise stillness, there may come a point when we experience a subtle shift of consciousness, which will reveal what is authentically manifesting around us, rather than what we think is there. It is important to tune into this level of information if we can, because we are not living in isolation but are part of the entangled interaction of all beings on this planet. It's an openhearted approach that will ultimately guide us towards spiritual enlightenment.

One of the energy wavelengths in a body is sound. So even in stillness there is sound that our soul listens to. The Universe has a musical resonance of souls.

Finding a quiet place can be a problem nowadays. According to the World Health Organisation, noise pollution is one of the most pressing threats to human health, second to air pollution. Noise can inflict physical and mental harm, not just to the ears, but to blood vessels and the heart too. Due to the sheer number of people affected by this problem, experts have recommended action should take place to reduce noise at source as well as designing society to be less noisy. For this reason I often now use earplugs when I am in busy public places to help keep my mind calm and untroubled by disruptive sounds. We also need to remember that noisy environments will adversely affect the health and wellbeing of animals as well.

Listening is part of looking

Being observant is an important aspect of listening. Animals are not misled by outer appearances, nor influenced by such limiting representations of other living things. Being observant means retaining an inner core of awareness so that our vision offers a sense of *feeling* what we are looking at, and really connecting with it, rather than being in a state of constant distraction.

As the Austrian poet and author Alfred Brendel succinctly points out: 'The word "listen" contains the same letters as the word "silent" ', reminding us that the two are interrelated. To this, I would add that the act of being consciously observant is an important aspect of both seeing and listening, whether we are paying attention to the visual world or to what we sense, feel and think. We don't need to try hard to be observant; it comes with intention.

We can hone this skill each day by taking time to look about us and noting what is going on wherever we live. If our view is devoid of greenery, we can perhaps look at the sky or at water. Even the cracks in a wall can be home to some form of life. By paying attention to our environment in this way, we are invited to contemplate the true nature of other beings, and the barriers between us will start to be swept away. Then we will find that we don't feel the need to alter or control the animals around us, for example, instead accepting them as our friends.

Noticing the invisible

The message of how to tune into animals, and therefore to all life around us, was reinforced for me by a pony. He was so very cute – a Shetland with tufts of shaggy hair sticking up on the top of his head and framing his ears. As soon as he knew I could hear him, the youngster had a lot to tell me; in fact the speed of his communication was highly amusing and I had to make notes quickly in order to keep up with him.

Unlike the pony, the man who was also there with us was unfocused and distracted – not for any particular reason that I could ascertain, but simply because he wasn't paying attention to his surroundings. As the man talked, his conversation drifted from one random topic to another, yet the pony offered a stream of succinct messages all relevant to the current circumstances.

Eventually the man blurted out, 'How can *I* hear what my pony is thinking and saying?'

At that exact moment, the wise pony looked up and snorted three times to show he had heard the man's plea and understood it. Quite clearly I heard the little horse's reply: 'Just listen! That's all you need to do.'

Then followed a lengthy discussion about how stressful modern life had become, with numerous distractions, little time to relax and a plethora of noise surrounding us. For all of these reasons, the man was adamant that he *couldn't* listen – but of course everyone can make lifestyle choices to create quiet periods for themselves. Rather than it being an elitist skill, we can all choose to listen. And once we really get the hang of it, we may find that we can listen to other beings even when in noisy places, because then we start to use our intuition to tune in, not our ears.

I often point out to people that if humans consider themselves superior to other beings, yet animals can tune into us so easily, then why should *we* find it so difficult? As the pony insisted, we just need to get on and do it! In her book *What Horses Say*, the late Julie Dicker described how, when she asked hundreds of horses the question, 'What would you like me to tell your human?' the majority of the horses replied: 'To observe us ... to listen to us.'

Having embarked on a path of listening to animals and nature, I enjoy it so much that I now absolutely need a quiet time every day – a window in which I can recover some peaceful headspace. Often involved in this process are relaxing activities such as embracing a cat, stroking a dog or standing by a dozing horse.

When we become quiet within, we may come to the understanding that we are not looking for external answers but that the real reward lies in looking within *ourselves* – where the secret key to everything that we are, and can be, lies.

Poppy helps

As humans, our most common way of communicating is with words, either spoken or written. However, animals don't pay much attention to words; instead they tune into our inner worlds, the state of which we mostly neglect to consider. Animals pay attention to our thoughts, emotions and intentions, as all of these possess energy vibrations that animals can 'read' and analyse. Adept observers, animals will also tune into other information such as the tone of our voice, our facial expressions, movements and posture. They will note the various smells released through our skin, wafting through the air. All of these clues are far more reliable indicators of what we are truly communicating than the words we use, which for animals can sit at odds with the other messages they pick up from us. It is perhaps not surprising that we sometimes find ourselves becoming annoyed and frustrated in situations where an animal doesn't appear to be listening to our spoken instructions.

Poppy, a seven-year-old Labrador, had a reputation for not listening. Out on walks Poppy would not only run off, but would leap at other dogs and tell them off before they got anywhere near her. It had become very stressful for her owner. The woman – let's call her Wendy – had consulted a behaviourist, who had offered tips on dealing with the dog's demeanour and attitude, which had helped to a degree; but generally the relationship between dog and human was not a close one. I soon concluded that the root of the problem lay with Wendy, who wasn't mindful of either her own actions or her thoughts; nor did she pay attention to the effect these had on her dog. Poppy was picking up on Wendy's inner state, which in turn acted as a set of instructions to the dog, who was only behaving in the way she thought she was being told to. Yet Wendy didn't have a clue this process was taking place.

It took some gentle discussion with Wendy for her to realise that the situation was more complex than just her dog being unruly. Eventually she talked about her personal life, how she lacked confidence and expected perfection in others as a means of self-approval. Admitting to low self-esteem, the woman hated not being in control of Poppy and considered it a sign of the dog's failure to like her.

I suspected that Wendy wasn't paying attention to Poppy as a sentient being in her own right, and was instead blaming herself that she had not trained Poppy to be better behaved; and that she was angry too that others had seemingly perfectly behaved dogs while hers was a hooligan! However, I wasn't making much progress with Wendy as I tried to explain about animals tapping into our inner focus, so Poppy helped me out. The woman had explained there were particular things that irritated her about her dog, such as not coming when called or refusing to stay still for very long. Indeed, so far during the consultation Poppy had paced around the room, occasionally trying to look out of a window or sniffing under a gap in a door – all signs of boredom. As Poppy paused and investigated my bag on a chair, I sent her a message:

I know you can hear me. Please can you come and sit by me so that I can talk to you? I want you to know that I will listen to what you have to say.

Poppy's ears pricked up; then she promptly came over to position herself by my feet, her back pressed against them. Wendy was intrigued, which gave me the opportunity to explain that I had noticed her sitting stiffly and that she was generating a somewhat unsociable ambience. Practising mindfulness techniques would not only encourage Poppy to want to be in Wendy's company, but would stand Wendy in good stead with other people too.

'But I don't know how to relax!' Wendy protested.

I pointed out that there was no need to worry as Wendy already had a great teacher – her dog, Poppy. It was important for Wendy to take time on a walk to enjoy their surroundings, and to note everyday things. If she saw someone approach with a dog, she was not to think, 'Oh no, Poppy is going to run at them, she's going to go mad, bark, jump up, be a nuisance. There'll be complaints, no one likes us, it's all terrible!'

This sort of thinking would, of course, act like a heap of instructions to Poppy to misbehave. Instead, I suggested that Wendy become observant of her surroundings in a positive way and when someone approached with a dog, she should say to Poppy something along the lines of: 'Wow, look at that beautiful tree, let's go check it out.' This would distract them both from potentially chaotic thought-processes, whilst simultaneously creating a more coherent emotional state.

In the weeks that followed, Wendy dutifully focused on improving her own disposition. As a result Poppy became much more inclined to avoid confrontation with strange dogs, and to pay attention to Wendy. It was lovely to receive this feedback from Wendy:

I realised how much the problem was related to my attitude. Now as we stroll along, I am listening, looking and being clear in my mind. Poppy has taught me to be more observant and to take pleasure in simple things, which I now know is important. By listening to her I know when to pause on walks and be in the moment. I suddenly feel really connected to Poppy.

As humans we need to pay more attention to life around us – a process that will eventually lead to our experiencing an intense sense of awareness and the realisation that we have invested in noticing the world as a whole. Listening and observing will strengthen our powers of insight, something which animals seek in their own lives as well as from us. If we are calm, as opposed to viewing the world from an agitated stance, the chaotic tumult in our mind will dissolve. The quieter we become, the more we can detect.

Some key steps to inner stillness

- Observe your inner state, including your emotions, thoughts, and your breathing. Tension on any level is a block to stillness.
- Meditation is known to reduce anxiety and a short period of silence allows us to create space for clarity of mind. Meditation does not necessarily mean sitting in a class whilst someone reads from a script. We can meditate more or less anywhere, by freeing ourselves to notice everything around us intensely, whilst simultaneously finding calm within.
- Practise channelling healing energy. The source of healing is the ultimate core of stillness. Healing energy is open to all, and is not dependent on belief systems. Animals are very receptive to a healing interaction. Chapter ten covers this in more detail.

When we observe the communication of animals through mindful awareness, we allow our intuition to escape from the mental prison that can otherwise hold us captive; and thus we start to perceive the lessons and insights that are being offered to us on a daily basis. Whether as guides in our daily lives, or occasional connections that we make, all animals can convey insights to help us. Once we are aware of this, we can actively seek ways to increase our ability to notice these communications, yet without wanting to make the process more beautiful. It is already perfect. It is not something we should seek to alter but which we should accept by acknowledging our place in the midst of the world – as opposed to following an isolated path, wearing sensory blinkers. This is where animal magic comes to our rescue. Listening to animals helps us to become better people-listeners too. Animals need us to get along with each other, to help each other and to understand human nature.

Communicating with a dog through using healing energy

Animals share with us this message:
'To hear us – listen in the space between minds.'

Meditating with animal friends

Meditation enables us to improve our observation skills and leads to a higher form of consciousness. We may think that we would like to reach this higher state yet believe that we are not spiritual enough or that it is too difficult to achieve. With a little bit of know-how anyone can do it, and the best teachers are the animals around us. Animals can lighten and brighten our mood any time we allow them to. Meditation helps to open up our sixth sense, which is important because it provides a platform for tuning into animals. There are various ways that we can learn to meditate, depending on our personal preference. Yoga-style meditation for example helps our posture, and when we feel comfortably relaxed in this way, it helps us focus on the meditative experience.

Welcoming a moment of peace

Why not try this simple exercise the next time you relax with an animal friend?

- Close your eyes, and take a moment to make sure you are sitting comfortably, keeping your arms and legs uncrossed.
- Move your head slowly from side to side and then back to face straight ahead, letting go of any tension in your neck.
- Raise and lower your shoulders, so that any stress held there is also released.
- Be aware of your breathing and follow your in- and out-breaths as you relax.
- Visualise a soft beam of pure white light coming down from above to the top of your head, then passing through your body to the soles of your feet.
- This light is warm, gentle and soothing. It connects you to a hub of consciousness.
- Now be aware of a bright blue light appearing before your face.
- Feel yourself drawn to this colour until you merge with it; then sense the light on your forehead.
- The blue filters into your mind and flows throughout your whole body. Allow yourself to relax more deeply until you sense a shift in your awareness – like a window opening in your mind.
- Take a moment to absorb the essence of peace from this place of increased awareness.

The animal or animals with you will be aware of the process that is taking place, and you may find yourself perceiving things as if from their viewpoint. The sensation may be fleeting or more prolonged. This is the vision of your sixth sense opening.

Resolving the mystery

The exercise on page twenty-nine allows our mind to freewheel so that it can listen more readily to the silent voices of animals. With practice, we can achieve this state of inner peace very quickly, leading to interesting insights that might otherwise be missed.

I was standing next to a horse once when the owner suddenly asked me who the horse liked best in the herd. Shifting my awareness, I put the question to the horse, and sensed the reply: 'Archie.' Turning to the woman, I told her that this was whom her horse preferred. The woman stared at me, one eyebrow raised slightly and I had the distinct feeling she thought I was being silly.

Saying she was mystified by my response, the woman added, 'Archie is a cat.'

At that exact moment there was a loud meow, and the horse quickly moved to hang his head low over the stable door. When I peered over the door, I saw a tabby cat standing on his back legs to rub his head along the horse's nose. And that cat's name, of course, was Archie.

In the conversation that followed, the woman admitted that her horse was not very settled in the herd, so it now seemed that he preferred the non-confrontational friendship of the cat. The woman admitted that she had been incredulous at my translation of her horse's message, and I was grateful that Archie had helped me out by appearing at that precise moment to confirm not only his existence but his role in the horse's life.

The small effort that it takes to embark on periods of stillness and pay attention to the wonder of the world around us, humming with life, often rewards us with enigmatic glimpses of invisible truths, which flash across the radar screen of our mind. From the mass of information that animals have shared with me, I am convinced that this is their domain of experience.

Stillness

- is not a void or emptiness. It is a place full of meaning, which reveals the knowledge we already hold within us.
- opens our eyes, mind, heart and ears to information from the invisible.
- helps us to sense the essence of silence. We discover what is important because we can now appreciate it.

- is a profound place of listening and observing. It elevates our awareness of all that there is.

The beauty of stillness is relevant to all species. Planet Earth needs us to become creators and caretakers of this state of peace.

Noticing what's there

The following exercise can help you to listen and observe, thereby connecting with your inner self and your external surroundings.

Stage one:
Animals can help you out with this exercise, but choose a time when your animal companion is resting so that you do not become distracted by activity. Settle yourself in the company of your chosen animal and begin by practising a few minutes of the breathing exercise on page 29. (You can notice your breathing pattern change again when you move on to stage two of this exercise.)

Stage two:
Continue to breathe evenly and deeply. Focus on a small area of your companion animal, such as a section of fur. Observe the appearance of the individual hairs. Are the hairs all the same length? Do they all grow in the same direction? Is the colour of each hair uniform all the way down the hair shaft? Are some hairs raised, or others flattened? How does the light fall on the individual hairs, and what minute flecks of highlighted colours do you notice?

Now gently touch the area and notice the texture and softness. Notice what you see and sense, but don't analyse the input.

When we focus on something intently in this way, it can lead to a quiet mind. Simply accept the information and let it flow into you, as a pathway of stillness opens in your mind.

A walk in nature offers many opportunities to meditate in a similar way on whatever we find there, such as a leaf or flower perhaps. We can, however, practise this exercise anywhere and with any object. I have done so on a plane and a train by focusing on my ring, taking in the curve of the metal, the glint of reflected light, noticing the patina of small marks and scratches on the band and the subtle irregularities of the stone set in the centre. Previously unsettled by travelling, my mind was calmed by the exercise, and then entered a state of mental clarity and alertness.

> Animals teach us that a combination of observation, listening and sensing create an invitation for contemplation.

The Japanese symbol for the word 'listen' is a pictogram formed from a combination of characters which can be translated as 'you', the whole person: undivided attention, eyes, ears and heart.

TO LISTEN

Ear 聽 You

Eyes

Undivided Attention

Heart

The Japanese pictogram for 'listen'

This is another example that encourages us to immerse ourselves in active listening, which means seeking to understand others by being non-judgemental and paying them our full attention, engaging in eye contact, empathy and without interrupting. All of which are behaviours that animals can teach us about. And let's not forget that the same concept applies regarding animals – so that we remember to listen properly to them and what they are communicating to us.

In the next chapter, animals show us the importance of opening the heart so that we can create a connection of loving attention with the world around us.

3. Open your Heart

I have never sensed anything with my brain, which is often busy thinking about what I feel, but I have felt a great deal with my heart.

There was an incident some years ago when a man jumped into a zoo moat to save a drowning chimpanzee. When asked why he performed this brave act, the man replied that he happened to look into the chimp's eyes and it was like looking into the eyes of a man. The message was, 'Won't anybody help me?'

Primatologist Jane Goodall referred to the incident during a lecture, noting, 'If you see that look with your eyes, and you feel it in your heart, you have to jump in and try to help.'

The man who jumped into the moat to help the chimpanzee was demonstrating unconditional love – helping because he felt the need to, without questioning it. When we open our heart then our eyes can see who animals are: sentient beings just like us although in a different form. Becoming champions of compassion and equanimity means that our heart energy is deep enough to love all creatures, no matter how seemingly insignificant.

Heart focused

Animals are masters of loving unconditionally – offering affection without any limitations, conditions attached or expecting anything in return. We talk about this as being an attribute of animals. Yet we are animals too, and to give love as a blessing to others is accessible to all of us. Although it is offered freely, without expectation, there is a reward for love given in this way, but it does not come in the form of dollar bills: such altruism creates space for soul enrichment, which, truth be told, is the only thing worth treasuring – as the man who helped the chimp showed to the world. Unconditional love is the song of the Universe; animals resonate with it whilst in the main humans pay heed to another tune, namely that of material gain or the self-serving ego. But it doesn't have to be this way, and it shouldn't be if we seek fulfilment and happiness. Droplets of continuous human compassion are needed to create an ocean of infinite peace. The animals are already making their contribution – they heal our hearts and nurture our souls.

Animals have helped me understand that within our heart we carry a blueprint shaped by our history, not just what we have done or where we have been, but our level of empathic kindness. It represents who we are at any given time. We manifest within our hearts the love we project. The heart is associated with intuition, and as animals are strongly attuned to their intuition, their link to heart intelligence makes sense. It is how they are able to gauge the energy of other species.

Animals have communicated to me that they measure our heart intelligence by the amount of light radiating from us. They see a ball of light in our heart area, which is larger the more altruistic we are. In contrast, the bigger our ego and the less benevolent we are towards others – not forgetting that nonhuman animals are 'others' too – the smaller the light. Our destructive actions or thoughts can cause this light to implode so that we possess darkness, something that animals can sense acutely. Given a choice, they want to move away from such individuals. Our intuition can also give us gut-feeling feedback in such situations, encouraging us to keep a distance too.

Inevitably, there will be situations that anger us and test our patience. A blip of exasperation or distress may pass through us, but animals can show us how to drown that out with light in our heart. Often, in their company, our good mood returns and we feel brighter.

Engaging the heart

Whilst we might think that listening is purely about clearing our thoughts and opening our minds, it also means engaging the heart and its intelligence. We now know that the heart is not just an organ, it is a place shown to contain memory cells, and I also believe it is where the soul resides. While the brain, it seems, is a powerhouse that controls our functions, the heart has the largest electrical field of all the organs in a body – one of the reasons why we sense and feel things there so intensely.

A type of heart-rhythm synchronisation can occur in interactions between people and their pets. During a study with a boy and his dog conducted by HeartMath director Dr Rollin McCraty, measurements were taken when the boy consciously felt feelings of love and care towards his pet. The boy's heart rhythms became more coherent and this change appears to have influenced the dog's heart rhythms too, which then became more organised. When the boy left the room, the dog's heart rhythms became much more chaotic and incoherent, suggesting initial separation anxiety. So here is evidence that hearts not only record information, but send out information for other beings to read – they're not just pumping machines.

Another study has concluded that the bond between owner and dog can be so strong that their hearts even beat in synch. Researchers at Melbourne's Monash University separated dogs from their owners, and via heart monitors strapped onto both humans and dogs recorded what happened when they were reunited. Initially both human and canine heartbeats quickly fell, but then began to mirror each other. Despite beating at different rates, the two hearts followed the same pattern, with the dog's heart rising and falling in tandem with the person's. The results of the study suggest that having a pet is good for not only our heart, but general wellbeing, helping us deal with the stresses of everyday life. As researcher Mia Cobb told *The Huffington Post*: 'If we can decrease our heart rate by hanging out with our animals, that's something that can really benefit the community.' This is an exciting discovery indicating wellbeing cohesion, a healing effect taking place as a result of interaction with animals.

In the course of my work, I've noticed that people often arrive for a workshop in a stressed or anxious state due to the pressures of modern life. However, as time progresses and we interact with the animals present, the change in atmosphere is remarkable, all due to the animals' healing heart presence. People start to get on better with each other and may even mention that they feel emotional as a heart-to-heart connection is enhanced. Profound insights are often sensed from the animals, inspiring people to make life adjustments and sometimes even change direction completely.

To be loved

It is important to love ourselves. The words of Buddha remind us of this: 'You, yourself, as much as anybody in the entire Universe, deserve your love and affection.' In order to understand love, we need to understand and love ourselves first, which might initially take practice and effort but which can then become second nature.

Animals just accept themselves and allow the experience of life to be one of continual learning and development. (Of course, when humans mistreat or harass animals they are tragically thrown into despair, which will in turn be reflected back onto those who mistreat them through the Universal laws of cause and effect.)

Animals offer companionship and encourage us to open our hearts so that we can see clearly and feel strongly. They allow us to explore our potential, which is why being with them is so easy. They teach us that it is through loving unconditionally we can feel most loved.

Lessons from a little cat

Sending out the vibration of love genuinely and unreservedly is essential for my work to have the best effect. Whenever I practise healing and animal communication, all of the things that I have learnt must come together – starting with meditation preparation, then letting go, listening and observing, and opening the heart. Animals find this energy attractive as it feels safe for them.

When people ask me what animals are the most difficult to work with, they expect me to name some exotic creature and are surprised when I reply, 'Cats'. Adept energy readers, cats expect respect, which may mean adapting a session to suit their terms, and it is not unusual for me to have to wait until they choose to respond during a healing session.

Girlie, a tortoiseshell cat, was very nervous when I first met her, having spent the early part of her life as a feral animal. One day, Chris and Elaine found her hiding in their garage and, being cat lovers, they started to put out food for their frightened visitor. It wasn't long before Girlie crept into the house and accepted their love and care, but her wild attitude of being alert for danger remained, and even now, as an old cat, Girlie was anxious around strangers.

Having cleared my mind of thought-clutter on the way to Girlie's home, I already had my breathing under control when she wandered into the kitchen – where she stopped in her tracks with a startled look on her face as soon as she saw me. Introducing myself, I explained to Girlie that I was there to help, and that she could direct the proceedings, which I hoped she would find acceptable. With this, I opened my heart and radiated unconditional love to her as a unique and special soul. A tell-tale shift in atmosphere filtered within me as our energies connected and blended. Girlie's stare widened, then she left the room with a sweep of her tail around the door. 'All in good time,' she seemed to be saying.

Going into the living room, I barely had time to make myself comfortable on the sofa before Girlie ran into the room, jumped up beside me and lay down. Staying mentally within a continuous stream of loving thoughts, I channelled healing to Girlie and observed her reactions. Quickly, she went into a trance-like state, eyes half open, her breathing slow and deep. I had made a deliberate decision not to touch Girlie but to offer healing with my hands off her body, as I felt that would be more tolerable for her. So I was very touched when she reached forward with a paw and placed in on my finger, clasping it.

Nearly an hour passed, during which healing energy extended into Girlie like spreading tentacles, and she ran through the gamut of relaxed body language, including snoring, rolling onto her back, and moving closer to touch me. Chris and Elaine commented on how they had never seen this trusting sort of behaviour from Girlie, apart from with them. Without a doubt, it was the result of my working from a core of unconditional love akin to the level so familiar to animals. It's important to stay in the loving moment, ratcheting up the healing intensity as the animal accepts our presence, and not becoming distracted, because if we lose focus they will sense it. It's like being a partner in a dance in which we move together as one, our hearts defining the rhythm of whatever takes place.

When I returned a couple of weeks later, Girlie was so excited to see me that she nearly fell over rubbing her body around me. She had a new gift of acceptance for me that day and, in the middle of a sleep, she reached up with a paw and tapped my hand as though giving me a high five. I knew then that I was part of her world and it was a very good feeling.

Girlie

If we approach animals with a loving, trusting heart they have the best chance of opening up to us. Adopting this stance generally in life helps us forge good relationships and friendships with people. Before I became

> Animals encourage us to unleash the heart. The potential of all that we can be lies within it. Intuition resides within heart energy and the mind is a satellite area of heart consciousness. Spinning out of control can occur in both the heart and the mind; balance and harmony emerge with love.

receptive to learning the myriad of lessons from animals, people sometimes called me aloof because of my acute shyness. They now comment that I am unrecognisable as the same person: time spent as a pupil of the heart with many thousands of animals has tempered my consciousness, as well as bringing me great happiness.

The love we have to share

Dust Bunny is an example of how a core of love keeps the flame of hope alive. I met the Pomeranian dog at Plavi Križ (Blue Cross) animal shelter in Croatia, where over seventy dogs and twenty cats were cared for; many had been amusing to people as puppies or kittens but later abandoned on the streets when they grew into adult animals. Having started their lives as the centre of attention, these animals then had to run the gauntlet of hatred and cruelty festering in some human hearts. Witnesses had seen Dust Bunny crossing a road when a man on a motorbike veered towards the little dog to run her over. No one went to help the stricken dog, assuming that she had been killed, and it was only some time later that an animal lover found the near lifeless animal lying in the gutter dirt, hence her being given the name Dust Bunny. A kindly vet had operated to repair the numerous fractures and crushed bones, and Dust Bunny became a permanent resident of the animal shelter. Recovery for Dust Bunny, however, was slow because as well as physical damage she was emotionally and mentally devastated.

When Agneza, vice president of the animal shelter, placed Dust Bunny onto my lap, the dog's small, twisted body relaxed and she dozed. After I had finished my healing connection, Agneza leaned forward to pick up Dust Bunny and it was then that I noticed a flame of love dramatically change the look on her face. I can only describe it as an outward manifestation of adoration. As Dust Bunny tilted her head to press it against the woman's cheek, the little dog's eyes contained an introspective expression of remembering why you love a person so much. Dust Bunny's body seemed to be glowing; in fact, the shimmer was so marked that I turned to see if a shaft of sun was shining into the room, but it was not. Woman and dog were as one, both giving and receiving love, and in that moment I was shown how happiness could evolve from devastation.

Agneza was the complete opposite to a person who hated life enough to want to destroy it, and it was clear that Dust Bunny's salvation lay in the love that humans shared with her. The healing energy created yet another turning point, because a few hours later Dust Bunny barked for the first time in the year that she had been at the shelter. It was as if she was saying, '*I have my voice back. Listen to me. The love we have to share makes life worth living.*' It isn't just about the giving of love, but how we receive it. Dust Bunny took the love offered and moved forward trustingly to savour life with her human angels.

Learning to trust again is something that most of us understand if we've been hurt in some way, and it features in Simone's story too. Having gone through some difficult times herself, Simone had nevertheless taken an abandoned dog into her heart. She told me:

> *The fact that my dog allows herself to be loved by me, to receive hugs and to trust after suffering, is very special. She is full of love and joy despite her past. When I realised that, I cried because I hadn't experienced so much unconditional love in my life before. I had lost a great part of my trusting heart and I have learnt from my dog to be at ease and more open to love and life. Her company teaches me to be joyful and grateful. My dog is a great friend and we have a soul-to-soul bond. I have a deep respect for her teaching.*

One of the key lessons offered to us by the animals in our lives is that if we don't have love, we don't have anything.

Close to us

The animals in our lives are often thought of as family members. Indeed, they may be the only family that some people have. Tearfully, Alexis confessed that coping with the illness of one of her cats was so traumatic that her heart felt like it was being crushed in her chest. 'I love my cats as my children,' Alexis told me.

I understand the depth of feeling many of us have for the animals in our lives, which does not diminish or detract from the love we have for humans; it is just different. I had to laugh, though, on hearing one woman say that no man had ever looked into her eyes with the loving adoration that her dogs did! During an event in Amsterdam, management executive Richard told me that whenever he sees a dog or cat he experiences an immediate uplifting sensation in his heart. I loved the way that Richard described this emotion as like a box being ticked, so enriched does he feel during such encounters, which soothe a stressful day. For my part, existence would be meaningless and empty without contact with animals. It helps build a sense of solidarity with all life, reminding us that we are not complete on our own and that our heart is expansive enough to embrace all species, and seeks to do so.

What can animals teach us about love?

Spirituality is being increasingly incorporated into business coaching. In Switzerland, I met Andreas Dudàs, founder of a global leadership training programme and an author. I asked him, based on his experience – his career managing billion-dollar projects, as a coach and through being with his own animal companions – what important life lesson he thought animals had to offer us. Right away he answered that it boils down to one thing: love.

As Andreas explained, many people in business feel that they have to play a particular role and thereby neglect to cultivate or heed their inner wisdom. They tend to focus on 'success', which often just creates stress. Moreover, there is a conflict in the business context in that people expect to be rewarded for whatever they offer, which is the polar opposite of giving love unconditionally. Sooner or later, though, in order to find the contentment that they are seeking, they need to open their heart. This leads to them engaging with, rather than fleeing, their feelings and starting to trust the intuitive self.

At the end of a day's work, Andreas is greeted at home by cats and dogs, whose projection of joyous love is immediately calming. He then wanders down to the horses, where, as he approaches, Andreas gets an overwhelming feeling that the horse is saying, 'Hey, I'm here for you. I don't need a reward, I am just giving from my heart.'

The world over, people can sense the unconditional pledge made to us by animals. We humans can do the same not just in a business context but in all aspects of our lives. When a human says, 'I love you', it often means something other than *I love you as a soul being* in the way that animals infer, because an agenda, ego, control, conflict or power can be attached to the words, or they might be uttered out of habit or just said for effect. This holds us back spiritually. If we followed the example of animals, genuinely engaging heart to heart, the planet would flourish and become harmoniously sustainable.

> Often the only way for us to express emotion is with an animal by our side, sharing the space of their all-knowing, openhearted love.

Following our heart

One evening, I gave a lecture in a beautiful art deco building in Zagreb and afterwards an eight-year-old girl called Jaga and her mother Martina came out from the audience to chat with me. They explained that they had enjoyed my pictures and stories, especially the ones about dogs, because they had been thinking about getting a dog in the future; then they went on their way.

A week after the lecture, I heard that Jaga had been so inspired that she had indeed persuaded her mother the time had come for them to have a dog in their lives. Mother and daughter subsequently went to an animal shelter in the city, but when they arrived Martina was astonished to see Jaga walk purposefully along the cages of dogs waiting to be homed, not stopping by any of them. The girl explained that she had a strong intuitive sense about a particular dog needing them. Stopping in front of a cage containing a brown dog with sad eyes and ears hanging down, previously overlooked by visitors seeking a pet, Jaga said with certainty in her heart, 'This is our dog.' The dog's sad demeanour immediately brightened and she wagged her tail. Those watching said it was as if the dog already knew the family, so easily and readily did she connect with them.

When I flicked through the photos that they sent me of that life-changing

> Give from your heart. This is where acts of kindness come from.

occasion, in the first photo I saw a miserable-looking dog in a cage and in the subsequent photos Jaga hugging a dog who is smiling. They took the dog home, called her Vivi and showered her with love and friendship. It's a wonderful example of following our heart and listening to the voice of an animal. As is so often the case when a heart-to-heart connection is made, words cannot adequately describe the feeling. It is simultaneously baffling, intriguing, exciting, calming and imperative.

Heart-to-heart conversation

A particularly profound insight about an aspect of love came from a horse. Anna had spent a year on a ranch where she had come across her dream horse, Duke. Although Duke had gained a reputation for bad behaviour because of his tendency to throw to the ground whoever got onto his back, Anna was drawn to him nevertheless. A loving bond developed between the young woman and the now gentle horse, and they enjoyed long trail rides together. When the time came for Anna to return home, thousands of miles away, she was devastated to leave behind her horse best friend. No doubt, anguish surrounding the parting would have hit Duke too, as he wouldn't understand why the one human who had shown him love and kindness had abruptly disappeared from his life. It was the end of a chapter in both of their lives.

For the past couple of years, Indy had been Anna's new horse. However, Indy didn't come anywhere near the benchmark set by Duke. In every interaction with him, Anna felt disappointment, and she consistently compared him unfavourably to Duke.

Unsurprisingly, a meaningful relationship did not exist between them, and finally Anna's mother called me in to help.

The day was breezy and fresh. However, I could see straightaway that both Anna and Indy seemed worlds apart as they wandered around the paddock together, as if each of them wanted to be somewhere else. Intuitively, I felt that what might unfold would be at the horse's invitation. Helping others to reach a place of understanding is what a teacher is required to do, and the educator today would be a horse.

After watching them together, I walked with Anna across a meadow beside the paddock. Although Indy had his head down to graze I noticed he was watching us at the same time, eyes turning in our direction. On reaching the fence I spotted a dandelion plant, the flower turned to a powder puff of seeds. I stooped to pluck it.

'Hold this and blow,' I said to Anna, 'and, as you do so, know that negative thoughts are flying away.'

In between puffs at the dandelion globe Anna talked about how she couldn't connect to Indy, explaining that the bond she so desperately craved was not there. 'He's not like my previous horse, Duke. Indy reacts in strange ways and I find myself saying to him: "*Why are you doing that?*"'

'Indy is a unique soul,' I reminded Anna, 'in the same way that there is no one else like you. How do you think Indy feels about being compared to another horse? As a sentient being, he senses that criticism from you. How would you feel,' I continued, 'if someone you wanted to have a close relationship with was constantly comparing you to someone else, belittling you as a person, not appreciating your value and generally cutting themselves off from what you were saying? Think about the confusion this creates.'

Anna didn't reply, her face contorted with emotion. I had inadvertently hit a nerve. It turned out that Anna's attitude related to her father who for years had compared her to other females, leaving her with a sense of inadequacy and bitterness. She had replicated this pattern of behaviour with Indy and now the realisation of what she had been doing shocked her. As the wind snatched the last fluffy bits of dandelion from Anna's hand and scattered them around us, I ventured, 'Are you able to tell Indy that you love him? But you have to feel it, it can't just be words, because he knows the difference between superficial and authentic. When Indy senses you sending him love, then you will be able to hear his messages.'

Anna closed her eyes and I knew she was reflecting on what was happening inside her. It had dawned on Anna that she should not be defined or shaped by another person's opinions of her. She was whatever she created inside herself. Several deep breaths followed as Anna cleared her mind and entered a state of passive acceptance, so that serenity could take the place of chaos. Opening her eyes, and reaching with her arms as though embracing the space between them, Anna called out to Indy that she loved him. At this outburst, the horse raised his head to look at her, his ears pricked. He was listening.

'I hear him now,' said Anna

'What is Indy saying?' I asked.

'His message is forgiveness. Forgiveness, he says, is … acceptance … and love.'

With this, Anna slipped under the fence and went towards Indy, halting a short distance away from him before dropping to her knees on the grass. Then something wonderful occurred – Indy stepped forward and pressed his face to Anna's heart area.

Anna explained what had taken place from her perspective: 'I could feel intense love flowing between us. Then Indy slowly walked away, leaving me with a deep feeling of bliss. And most importantly the knowledge that he had forgiven me through his love.'

Connecting soul to soul

A trip to wonderland

In my early days of spiritual development, I had an experience related to the lesson that Indy offered Anna. During a meditation session, the tutor asked us to include an animal in our meditative thoughts. I chose to think about a rabbit because at the time I had a pet rabbit called Terry. Drifting into contemplation, I followed Terry in my mind as he hopped around my garden. Then Terry disappeared into a wild area, and my meditative focus remained on him even though I could not 'see' him.

With a sort of whoosh, I suddenly found myself entering what I can only describe as another dimension; it was like looking into an empty space but with heightened senses. In that moment, something clicked in my being, and I understood everything in relation to a situation that had been troubling me. Simultaneously I felt overwhelming love within and around me, finding that it gave me no option but to forgive a particular person who had upset me. It was all done in a flash – the emotional baggage dissolved.

My rational mind then interfered with the flow by trying to make sense of what was going on, and the sensation shifted. I dropped out of that amazing weightless state and in my mind's eye Terry was there again, facing me now, his nose twitching and a clump of grass protruding from his mouth. Later that day, when I got back home, I thanked him profusely because I knew he had played a role in the revelation, helping me come to terms with a situation that had previously seemed insurmountable. The experience also showed me that animals must operate from this expansive perspective, viewing situations from a place of empathy in its purest form.

We have a lot to learn from animals about unconditional love

Heart of hearts

Animals demonstrate that they can maintain effortless coherent alignment between their hearts, minds and emotions. All without having to meditate – and that's an enviable skill! By tuning into animals, we can absorb their heart aura, which will in turn help to activate our own senses fully. When such a connection takes place, people often comment that their 'heart has a funny sensation' or they feel emotional. This is the result of heart-to-heart coherence taking place. Not only do the two hearts connect, but our own heart links inwardly to our mind and emotions; therefore general energetic synergy also occurs. This sort of co-operation helps the heart's rhythms to stabilise themselves, enabling the body's physical processes to be in synch with each other, thereby contributing to the optimal functioning of the brain. Mental clarity combined with optimal heart rhythm performance is ideal for augmenting our intuitive process.

> Forgiveness is something that we all need, whether self-forgiveness or from others. A cloud lifts and calm infuses our being. We feel loved, nurtured, safe and happy.

As we've seen, our hearts and our intuition are inextricably linked – and when we give them free expression the rewards they offer are immense. It seems that when we set ourselves free to love unconditionally, forgiveness is included in that gift. I once read that the only love we keep is the love we give away. This is a great description of loving unconditionally: the effect reverberates back to us, because through loving in this way we find ourselves within a cocoon of benevolence.

4. Be Aware

'The mind that perceives the limitation,
is the limitation.'
Buddha

Before life became so complex and frantic, our ancestors had time to pay attention to the Universe's messages, a skill that has become lost in today's hectic world. I have increasingly come to understand that animals are not limited by a closed mind, which can be a human failing. Again and again during the course of my work, I find myself taking a peek into the depth and breadth of animal awareness, and this has created in me a hunger to expand my own sensory antennae and to become more attuned to my surroundings.

But first – an interruption. Just as I was sitting down to write this section of the book, my husband called me from outside. Looking through the window, I spotted the face of a dog peering out of the car, and my husband explained that as he was driving home from the grocery store he came across the animal running down the road in an obviously distressed state. In both our vehicles, we keep a box containing a dog leash, doggy treats, old towels and a horse halter and rope. If we then come across a situation where an animal needs help, we have some rudimentary items with us that we can use.

My husband explained that he had pulled over and parked safely some way ahead of the scared, fleeing dog. Then he had spoken to it in a friendly way whilst rattling a bag of treats. Thankfully, the dog, a muddy spaniel, stopped panicking. When my husband opened the car door, she jumped in to lie down on the soft towels, panting hard but happy to be stroked and rolling onto her back. And now we needed to find out where she lived.

I went out to sit in the car with the dog. She soon understood that I was aware of her thoughts and could hear her inner voice. After telling her that I would help to reunite her with her humans, I asked, 'Where have you come from?' Sceptics may scoff at this, yet I have found that animals possess an existential energy map that includes a link to their home, and the communication that came to me was that the dog lived close by.

This need not have been the case, because we live in a rural area where animals are sometimes dumped by heartless people who want to rid themselves of these innocent beings who seek only our love and care. Sadly I have been involved in some of these cases, the most recent concerning an elderly Siamese cat who was dumped with no identification in a small cage at the edge of a car park. Cold, hungry, frightened and upset, the cat had clearly been deliberately abandoned, and, I sensed, had been driven a long way to ensure that returning him was not an option. Thankfully the cat quickly found a home with a very special local person with whom he could live out the rest of his days in comfort.

During a subsequent healing session with the cat, now called Woody because he'd been found by a copse, he made me aware of what had happened to him and why. He had been happy in his previous home for a while; then loud voices and violent arguments developed between the couple that he lived with. One day, he saw suitcases in the hall, and with sadness watched the woman grab them and walk out. Hours later, he found himself shoved into the cage and transported hundreds of miles in a car, the man driving, to then be left shivering in the car park.

In cases like this, a healing consultation is similar to working with a person suffering from post-traumatic stress disorder (PTSD), in that the animal is in shock and needs to find a way of releasing the energy of its distress. With the help of energy healing, Woody was able to recover quickly from his ordeal and settle happily into his new caring home, with lots of cuddles to show him just how much he was loved and a special place in the garden to doze in the sun.

But back to the lost dog – as she leaned her head across my arm, intuitive awareness directed me to the northwest area of the next village as being where she had come from. We set off in that direction, but, having stopped and asked a few people if they knew the dog and where she lived, drew a blank. The logical next step was to call into the local vet and see if the dog had a microchip. Thankfully she did, and a few minutes later the owners had

49

been identified and were on their way for a joyful reunion with Susie, as we now knew her name to be.

Susie was less than a year old and had bounded off to chase a young deer, following a trail that led out of the safe woods and onto a busy road. Frightened by the traffic, Susie had run blindly for a few miles in the opposite direction to her home until my husband had passed by – and now all had ended well.

Animals show us how to open our senses to the environment

Paying attention

As Susie's story suggests, we live within an incredible storehouse of information and making a deliberate effort to become aware of it is much better than blundering through life. A strong and rapidly growing database on animal sentience supports the notion that a wide variety of species experience emotions ranging from joy and happiness to deep sadness, grief and PTSD, along with empathy, jealousy and resentment. Science has shown that mice, rats and chickens, for example, display empathy, and countless other

> There is an
> important spiritual
> awareness that evolves within
> the souls of people when they
> develop a deep connection
> with the Universe. They then
> begin to appreciate how a
> spark of the Universe lies
> within each one of us.
>
> This knowledge helps our
> souls to vibrate in harmony
> with other beings.

'surprises' are rapidly emerging. When we glimpse the realities of animals' inner worlds, this comprehension changes our perspective in turn, and leads to greater wisdom. By paying more attention to the life around us, we begin to experience intense moments of awareness that connect us to the world as a whole, and develop an appreciation of our planet as a dynamic energy centre supporting billions of lives, most of which are nonhuman.

In order to develop awareness we need to have empathy: the ability to see the world as someone else does through understanding and sharing their feelings. If we can empathise with another person's feelings in any given moment, it will be easier to understand why their actions seemed logical to them. Being empathic likewise helps us to communicate in ways that make sense to others, as well as be receptive to communications that are directed at us. This is a foundation of social interaction, and our relationships with animals should be included in the loop of empathy.

Some people have only a tiny amount of natural empathy, while there are those who have an excellent ability to pick up on how others are feeling just by being near them. Most people are mid-range, though, aware of how others might be feeling only part of the time. Fortunately we can improve on this with the help of animal teachings. Using techniques that we glean from the example of animals will help us to orienteer ourselves in the Universe and become more self-aware.

Every living being has Planet Earth in common. But by trying to fit everything into our human-designed systems and agendas, we set up nature to fail, creating instead a mirror image of our human inadequacies. Our human tendency to attack or destroy anything that does not suit us – even though these actions ultimately diminish, deplete and weaken our environment – contributes to our twenty-first-century disconnection from nature and is detrimental to our wellbeing.

Yet in some respects we live in enlightened times, as increasing numbers of us do value and appreciate all the world's creatures for their intrinsic beauty and majesty. When we open our eyes to our environment, we find ourselves surrounded by an incredible diversity of life – from the depths of the oceans to the sky and everything in between. Modern research, for example, has shown that whales are placid, sentient animals with a highly developed awareness of their own selves. Indeed, it has been suggested by cetacean expert Hal Whitehead that whales might have their own elementary concept of religion. This means they possess complex qualities of awareness. Scientists have even found that insects seem to display rudimentary self-awareness and personality traits. Researchers at Queen Mary University of London have discovered that insects can learn complex skills and improve upon them. The scientists showed for the first time that bees could learn by watching and rather than copy what they saw, change it to make it better – a skill only previously seen in humans, primates and certain marine mammals. Project supervisor Professor Laras Chittka said: 'Our study puts the final nail in the coffin of the idea that small brains constrain insects to have limited behavioural flexibility and only simple learning facilities.' This reinforces to us how complex all life forms are, no matter how small. Nothing is insignificant.

Likewise, when I come across questions such as 'do animals know who they are?' I have only to reflect on the thousands of varied animals that I have met during the course of my work, all of which have diverse thought processes. These days, ever-increasing numbers of TV programmes such as *Planet Earth* and *The Blue Planet* are revealing just how much foresight and planning animals are capable of.

Nevertheless, various – to my mind, flawed – scientific tests have been undertaken to try to ascertain if certain species are self-aware. The 'proof' in these sorts of tests often depends on whether or not an animal can recognise him- or herself in mirrors, as animals such as chimpanzees that can recognise themselves in reflective surfaces are traditionally said to be able to conceive of their identity. But these tests are not infallible because we cannot judge animals by our own limitations. For example, animals don't need mirrors to know who they are, and as mirrors are not a naturally occurring phenomenon, using them as the definitive scientific measurement tool sets up animals to be unsuccessful.

When doing their research, scientists need to take into account the role of all of the senses in addition to vision, which is not so key for certain species. Some animals, such as rodents for example, can distinguish among individuals yet don't seem to respond as strongly to visual prompts as other mammals do. For many animals, sounds and smells are more important building blocks when it comes to constructing their understanding of the world.

Animals teach us the importance of exploring our senses

And while we are on the subject of animal sentience, let's not forget the sixth sense. Human civilisation today does not set great store by the concept of the sixth sense, which we have consequently allowed to become weak and flimsy – whilst other species have honed theirs to perfection. In my experience, animals, birds and insects are all adept at using the sixth-sense level of awareness and might well wonder why we insist on sticking mirrors in front of them to try to find out if they are self-aware; perhaps they are even wondering, 'Why are you so confused about the complex strata of sentient awareness – and what on earth has a mirror got to do with it?'

Animals possess an intrinsic intuition about the unity connecting everything. And so do we – animals simply guide us to become conscious of what we already innately know in our soul.

Unfortunately, the argument put

forward by some – that animals are not as aware as humans are – can be used to defend the sorts of treatment that animals are often subjected to, such as intensive farming and laboratory testing. Yet animals are in many ways more aware than we humans are and need our protection as never before, so that not only can they survive but we humans can learn more about who *we* are too.

Thankfully things are now moving on apace. In the summer of 2012, an international group of neuroscientists gathered together in Cambridge, England, to lend their weight to a radical idea. The conference attendees, including theoretical physicist Professor Stephen Hawking, listened to around fifteen presentations and closed the day by endorsing a statement composed of 612 decisive and carefully chosen words – which in effect announced that many of our fellow animals, including all mammals and birds, also have consciousness.

Those of us who have spent time with pets, horses or other animals, or who embrace the fight for animal rights, might perhaps utter an underwhelmed sigh at such statements. But this occasion was different due to the high profile of the scientists present and their game-changing declaration that: '*Humans are not unique in possessing the neurological substrates that generate consciousness.*' When it comes to the anatomy, chemistry and physiology of our brains and the way these interplay within our consciousness, they said that we are not alone.

At the conference, an important element of consciousness was nevertheless overlooked, perhaps as being a step too far for the scientists: soul awareness. I believe this is the hub that really holds consciousness. True awareness taps into a primordial, endless state of being, thereby affording us insights into the whole of knowledge – something that our animal teachers are adept at accessing. The more that we know about them, the more this facility of theirs is coming to light.

We are aware of our consciousness (the 'I' that we are), and so are other sentient beings. However, consciousness is not tangible and whilst we may consider that frustrating, other beings do not because they don't over-analyse things. Like many other people, I've long thought that the animals' approach must make for a peaceful state of existence, which is one reason why they are often so healing to be with. Because the soul is aware and we are soul beings, there is no distinction between consciousness and awareness. The two words can be treated synonymously and used interchangeably.

But to go back to that day in Cambridge: the scientists at the conference planted an historic flag with their statement, and sparked a global enquiry into the ways in which we should treat animals, and, beyond that, into the meaning of life itself. The concluding statement was placed firmly on the wall, indicating that we can learn what we seek to know about life – from animals. Having been given permission to ask about our connection to animal sentience, and to seek answers, we find ourselves engaging with people who are part of this awareness revolution. We are all being invited to take part in a new groundswell of enlightened thinking.

A mysterious incident

One of my favourite ways of relaxing is by going to music events, including in Salisbury Cathedral, near where I live. Architecturally spectacular, it has the tallest spire in England and the acoustics are wonderful. Throughout the year performances of varying types are laid on and this particular occasion featured a concert performed by the Royal Philharmonic Orchestra. In the setting of the magnificent arches of the cathedral, the music was mesmerising, yet I nevertheless found my thoughts straying to concerns about a turbulent family situation. Shuffling in my seat, I was annoyed with myself for losing focus.

During the interval, I wandered over to the cloisters, where I came across a TV monitor showing live images of a nest of peregrine falcon chicks situated near the top of the cathedral spire. After a few minutes spent watching the screen, I heard a screech from above. Upon looking across the cloister garden, I was rewarded with a view of a parent falcon soaring in the sky, before landing on a ledge near to where the nest was situated.

It was at that moment that I became aware of a man standing next to me, who said, 'I love coming here to watch the birds.' Turning, I saw a thin, middle-aged man in ragged clothing, with a weather-beaten face and piercing bright-blue eyes. The man's appearance struck me as reflecting a life bereft of luxuries, but his eyes sparkled with wisdom and compassion.

The man continued talking, telling me that he visited the cathedral most days to watch the pictures of the nest and observe the parent birds flying, hunting and feeding. He shared some scientific facts about peregrine falcons, and how that data related to this particular family of birds. After a pause, he mentioned he'd lived on the streets for over twenty years. During that period, having all the time in the world to study his surroundings, he had developed an acute sense of awareness.

'I study the wildlife and pets that I see, people too,' the man murmured. 'I notice how we can miss things by not paying attention. These past years have made me realise that animals and birds are very important teachers. We need them in our lives for our survival, and I wish everyone knew who animals are.'

During this brief encounter, I stood in rapt attention as I listened to an eloquent and insightful address from someone whom I recognised as a kindred spirit. I was stunned that this man used the phrase 'who animals are', aware that each animal is a unique individual. Many humans, however, unfortunately do not incorporate this truth into their mindset.

A bell rang, announcing the second half of the concert, and, as suddenly as he had appeared, the man moved away, quickly swallowed up by the crowd returning to their seats. I briefly wondered if the man had been real or perhaps an apparition. But my sister came along at that moment and asked me who the man had been that she had noticed talking to me.

I have since pondered over why I had that chance meeting; in a crowded building, what brought me and the homeless man together? It was, of course, the animals. When we champion the rights of animals, then we find that we receive disclosures from animal voices through human messengers. We attract others on a similar wavelength through our collective awareness and these people will engage us in relevant conversations. More than that, we come across a great many animals who want to talk to us when they know that we are choosing a path of elevated consciousness. Animals need us to get along with each other, to help each other and to understand human nature. That night at the concert the animals had sent a powerful message – and I liked the feeling of recognition. I sensed too that my awareness had gone up a notch. People and animals come and go in my life, leaving me with cameo impressions of spiritual intimacy, so that I will always remember them for what they've taught me.

Awareness is knowing

One bright and sunny spring morning, I met twelve-year-old Jamie and his shaggy mixed-breed dog, Billy, whose first message to me was that he was the boy's healer. Billy continued by saying that he loved Jamie very much, but his communication came with a strong sense of sadness coupled with a feeling of betrayal.

When I mentioned this to Jamie, his eyes brimmed with tears and he cried, his small shoulders hunched and shaking. It is particularly distressing to see a child weep and I was unsure whether to continue, but, when I checked with Jamie's guardian, she urged me to help. The message from Billy reflected exactly how Jamie was feeling: bullied at school, he confided that he felt stuck in a hopeless situation. Jamie even considered himself to be a failure as a person. Pushing a hand nervously through his hair, Jamie then whispered that he had only recently been informed that the man he'd always called his father was in fact his stepfather, his biological father having left Jamie's mother before he had been born. It had been a traumatising discovery and the emotional repercussions were difficult for the boy to endure.

We discussed the situation for a few minutes and throughout this time Billy intently watched Jamie. That familiar energy connection encircled me, and, listening in a latitude that I call 'the space between worlds' – between visual and invisible realities – I could sense the dog showing me a scene related to Jamie. In the quick-fire way in which information comes to us when we listen to the voice of animals and we prepare ourselves to translate the messages on their behalf, I knew that the image was connected to something that Jamie had very recently been part of. The image that appeared in my mind was seen from Billy's perspective, a kaleidoscope evolving from blurred to focused, showing Jamie looking intently at a field with notebook and pencil in his hands.

'So what was the significance of the tableau that I was being shown?' I asked Jamie. A smile lit his face and he chuckled.

'That's so amazing,' he laughed, 'because this morning I took part in a school nature study with some friends. It was in a field behind my house and I didn't realise Billy was watching me. I'd no idea he was aware of what I was doing.'

The truth is that we are constantly on the radar of animals. Even if they are not part of our day-to-day lives, animals know everything about us just by reading the map of our energy field. Billy wanted Jamie to know that he studied the boy's every action as his canine witness. By revealing how much he was aware of what Jamie did and by bothering to observe his actions, I felt Billy achieved more that day than a human therapist could have done to make the boy feel important and cared about.

Animals teach us to project love and consideration to all other beings. This act reflects back to us and our increased consciousness can then enable us to enjoy being loved in turn.

Animals show how the act of loving generates yet more love, like a giant spotlight radiating positive energy to encompass an ever-expanding circle of beings.

Touch aware

Whenever we touch, our awareness absorbs information. As we focus on this sense, we often find that our mind will clear itself of unwanted clutter and the stress of day-to-day problems, enabling us to feel calmer.

Water is a tactile medium that you can easily experience for yourself, either by standing in shallow water or running a hand through it. The next time you do, focus your attention and slowly elevate your mind to the level of tuning into water as an element. Can you sense the water molecules responding to the light? In your mind's eye 'see' the shapes of the molecules (each one is unique in form) sloshing about your feet or hands.

Through your contact with the water, project your thoughts in order to sense how water feels to the millions of creatures that live in this element. Perhaps one or two particular creatures will come into your mind more strongly than others. Enjoy whatever experience comes to you for its own sake, as a unique gift. As a species, humans are often keen to analyse everything, missing the moment whilst scrabbling about for a meaning, rather than simply accepting what's there as an experience in its own right.

As an awareness exercise, connecting to the earth is also valuable, and in spiritual practices we often talk about 'being grounded' or 'earthing'. Weather permitting, it's beneficial to spend a few minutes as often as possible standing or walking barefoot. During this time, we might ask ourselves how the surface feels next to our skin; what sensations the grass offers us; how the animals feel when they move over the ground, unfettered by clothing. When we feel the texture of the ground under our feet, we can imagine Earth energy replenishing us. We can also repeat this exercise when paddling in water.

Self-awareness through horses

Because they are prey animals, highly reactive to energy on both seen and unseen levels, horses offer helpful lessons by reflecting what's going on in our psyche. Sometimes during my equine workshops, students come up to me and say that this or that horse does not want to be involved, because whenever the student approaches the horse, the horse then moves away. I make sure only to use venues that provide a horse-friendly lifestyle, and work with carers who are thorough about checking their horses daily for pain and illness, so in these situations, I am fairly confident the real issue isn't quite what's being described to me. All the same, I will always assess the horse in question for a sudden onset of problems. However, in all but a couple of cases, the lack of connection on the part of the horse was because the human was not self-aware.

Despite a morning of meditation and discussion about inner stillness and other vital ingredients for creating the sort of energy that will encourage a horse to want to be with us, it seems that some people do not quite manage to let go of unresolved emotional baggage or self-limiting beliefs. If this happens, we then work on paying attention to the inner self, which means that we consciously tune into proactively working from the position of our Higher Self. This allows us to truly observe our actions, thoughts, feelings and decisions so that we can accept who the horse before us is as a sentient being, rather than remaining stuck in our own world of worries.

Then, as if by magic, those seemingly uninterested horses will step forward and peacefully stand with the person who was having difficulties.

It is usually an emotional eureka moment, especially because a shift in awareness changes us for the better. In making the conscious decision to hear the horse's story, we learn how to witness who they are as individual beings. Horses like that. Reflected towards us in return are their bountiful teachings in sensitivity, which we need in order to nurture our awareness.

An equine greeting

Wildly aware

Nature's signs are all around us, and we can work with this bounty to create our own platform of mindful awareness. If you take a walk and find yourself stopping to look at a small flower, for example, almost hidden at the base of grasses rustling in the breeze, consider its symbolism – which might otherwise be overlooked if you are only taking in the expansive view. And, even though you cannot see them, be aware of the multitude of animals who know that you are there.

Becoming naturally attentive

Choose a safe spot, then sit quietly and observe what's going on around you. Watch how creatures interact with each other and their habitat. It's amazing what nature will reveal.

Resist an impulse to get too close, to reach out, or call out to wildlife. Use binoculars and telephoto camera lenses instead if necessary. The best chance of observing nature is to become as insignificant as possible, but stay safe. Retreat immediately if an animal approaches you or shows any sign of aggression. Remember that you have intruded into their habitat, and wild animals can feel threatened by this, and this can apply to domestic animals too.

Large wild creatures aren't as abundant as smaller ones, so it can be especially rewarding to look for them. However, interest, like beauty, is largely in the eye of the beholder. A fly is as significant to the planet as an elephant is.

Contemplate each creature's role in the bigger picture as a potential model for human society and consider what lessons we might learn from them.

Absorb information from the animals, birds, insects and aquatic creatures, and make notes about what you sense or feel as your awareness expands. Perhaps you will be inspired to write down a message that comes to you from the collective consciousness of life?

Cherish the knowledge and wisdom of the creatures living around you, whether you can actually see them or not. Note any sights and sounds you experience – the call of a bird, animal tracks, scattered leaves, seedlings popping out of the ground, a flower unfurling. Indulge your curiosity.

Learn from animal friends by watching their actions and reactions and adjusting your internal state accordingly. Your awareness expands as you discover how much they can teach you about yourself.

61

Lessons from a lone wolf

Many of us carry an ancient longing to get away from the material world and return to live in nature, but most of us of course can't pursue this feeling. However, we can conjure up what it would be like, and stepping out into nature is where we can become aware of the wisdom of the wild – as this next encounter proved for me.

I was tired. Not the all-consuming, overwhelming, debilitating tiredness of stress, illness or relationship issues, but the fatigue that comes from giving something your best effort, focusing intently. I had been teaching for two days in Alberta, Canada and after saying goodbye to everyone, my husband and I took a short drive into Banff for supper. As dusk fell, my day was blessed by the sight of a badger crossing the road in front of our car, before disappearing into the undergrowth. It was a quick glimpse but enough for me to see that this badger was very different from those I am used to seeing in my garden in England. There, the badgers are black and white, while the Canadian species that crossed our path was brown and white, with a flatter head than its European cousin. It was a great start to the evening.

A few minutes later, as we passed down a narrow track, I was startled to see what appeared to be a horse staring back at me from a copse of trees. A similar creature with antlers a few feet away gave me a clue; we had come across a herd of elk, moving like ghosts through the woods. Later, as we turned into the driveway of the cluster of log cabins where we were staying, a much larger 'ghost' filled my vision. A bull moose, who then faded into the night, leaving a sense of his omnipresence in the space before us.

Our plan for the next day was to drive to a national park and we found a map in a visitor centre indicating a little-used dirt road, which in fine weather made for a passable, if slow and dusty, two-hour drive back to civilisation. Given the infrequent traffic, there was a better chance of seeing wildlife along it, and, sure enough, about an hour into the drive, I spotted what looked like a large dog ahead of us on the track. I glanced around for signs of human habitation but wilderness lay all around, and I assumed that so far from civilisation this animal must be a coyote. We stopped the car, turned the engine off and waited for the animal to move away, but, untroubled by our presence, it instead came towards us, right down the middle of the track.

The dog-like animal moved in a curve from the centre of the road to the verge by the roadside, but kept up the same momentum, trotting along, head turning this way and that, obviously knowing where he was going. My camera was on the back seat of the car in a bag, and to get it would have meant crashing around over seats, so I decided to stay put and imprint the encounter into my memory. Besides which, I have learnt over the years that often when you take a photo, you risk missing a special moment of pure connection that enables you to fasten the moment firmly in the mind, where it can be revisited and relived at will.

Then it dawned on me – this was no coyote but a large, lone, male timber wolf. I was so excited in that moment that my heart raced and a shiver ran down my spine. Oh goodness me! I felt suddenly transported into another world, with my heightened senses whirring away. I took in every detail of the wolf's appearance as he drew closer. The colour striations of his body fur, the swing of his tail, how the hairs of it feathered outwards, the effortless light rhythmical loping of his legs, the ear carriage and beautiful head. By now the wolf was almost level with our car and about to pass by as I sat there, my excited face pressed to the window.

Then it happened. As the wolf drew level with the car, he paused; it was only for a second or so, but nevertheless he stopped, turned his head and looked right at me. Two golden-brown eyes bored into my own, and we locked into a mutual consciousness. In that moment I was dancing soul to soul with a wise being whose awareness far surpassed anything that a mere human could possess. The wolf knew everything that was truly important; ancient wisdom was flowing through him, passed down through the generations and not forgotten or set aside. His awareness was vivid and buzzing with intensity – information about the machinations of the whole Universe, weather systems, energy fields, interspecies communication, nurture, life, love and death. That look said to me, 'I am aware of everything.'

The wolf possessed the wisdom of the world and his gaze is forever imprinted within me. In some way, the wisdom that he transmitted is imprinted there too, although it is too intensely expansive for me to be able to describe. I just know that within me is the wolf's awareness. Although the wolf only paused in his stride, our actual connection seemed frozen in time, like pausing a film on TV. It seemed that the lesson was so important it had to be highlighted in a cosmic spotlight. Then the wolf turned away to continue his journey.

I called out to his disappearing frame, 'Wow, you beauty, bless you for this incredible insight!'

The encounter certainly shifted the energy within me, because you can't meet a master teacher and not learn something meaningful and prophetic. Even if this is merely that we humans have such a lot to learn that one lifetime isn't enough. Often, catching me unawares, I get a sense in my mind's eye of that wolf looking at me – into me. I am comforted that through the now proven scientific fact that we are all connected, he knew me. We met and so are forever linked, as I am to every creature whose soul has touched mine.

> Being aware of the core of who you are means paying attention to your thoughts, the things that you do, what you feel and why, your integrity towards other beings, as well as your ability to be a witness of the world of other creatures. Paying attention to these things is something that animals can help us with so that we can simplify our lives, ditch our destructive ego-driven behaviour and move towards who we would like to be. It is spiritual evolution.

So what lessons evolved for me that day through my wolf encounter? In the realm of animal symbolism, the wolf offers some of the most striking meanings. These include instinct, intelligence, wisdom and awareness of the importance of social connections. It became clear to me that, when a wolf shows up in our life, its message reinforces our need to pay attention so that we can expand our awareness towards achieving the depth and breadth of knowledge about our planet that animals possess.

5. Understand

I have looked into the eyes of animals and in return they have contemplated me with curiosity and awareness, convincing me of their sentience – their great intelligence, wisdom, understanding and sense of purpose.

For years when I was a child, well into my teens, I used to suffer from a bewildering sense of not understanding my purpose in life and would often ask my mother, 'Why am I here?' – a question that she found strange and perplexing. Later, at college, the topic of our existence on Earth was something I enjoyed vigorously debating with fellow students. Was there a grand plan that we needed to get to grips with, which somehow added value to our time here? Or was it OK to live without consideration of anyone or anything else? The animals in my life at that time must have thought that I was making a meal of something quite easy to grasp, if only I looked in the right place!

The answer to my musing didn't materialise, though, by dropping out of the sky, appearing in a dream or being written one morning on my bathroom mirror. Spiritual clues did arrive, but while I was trying to work out how my life should have meaning I became distracted by material attractions – and so it became a frustrating exploration. I intuitively felt that it was worthwhile searching for a sense of purpose in life, and that the varying aspects of existence were somehow interrelated. However, the meaning of it all lay beyond my grasp at the time, no doubt because I needed to have more interaction with animals.

Gradually it dawned on me: beings other than humans held the answer to my quest. I needed to pay attention to all the life around me. Animals, it seems, inherit an innate sense of purpose, which drives their actions and sense of fulfilment. Our situation is different from theirs in that we acquire ideas about our purpose in life from other sources as well as our genes, such as our conditioning, our family, country or religion. These may not suit us, though, leading to feelings of inner conflict and spiritual discomfort. Seeking understanding for ourselves can draw us away from society's dogmas.

One of the things I discovered was that, given the choice, animals will usually strive to make the best use of their time rather than waste it. They are naturally driven to use their time to fulfil a specific purpose and their example encourages us to be perceptive and conscientious so that we too project harmonious energy.

Through studying animal behaviour, I realised that animals intuitively understand about the integration of communities and the divergence of species. They readily slot into a purpose within their society. However, humans have never really got to grips with this concept, instead creating single-minded and insular ways of living, leading to fractured societies. We have much to learn about getting along, whereby each member of the community is content to fulfil a unique role which does not destroy the critical balance of the whole.

Our behaviour has a knock-on effect not just in our own life but all around us, and can create a reverberation that continues for eternity. We can change our ways at any time so that the hectic energy ripples we create become calmer. Tuning into animals helps us cultivate new pathways of knowledge whereby we can access our inner strength, liberating us from the pressures of time – as though we have more of it and it is of a better quality.

The urge to fly

The following experience drew me a little further into the complex matrix of reality that we inhabit. Just when I had considered myself to be doing OK in terms of spiritual understanding, I was shown how fragile my grasp was relating to the cognizance that animals possess. Venturing out into what seemed like a mundane day became a glorious classroom.

The air was full of birdsong as I stepped out of my car, and, looking up at the bright blue sky, I noticed that it was speckled with hundreds of house martins and swallows – hence the glorious sound. Back at home, I'd witnessed a similar scene before setting out: the gathering of local birds in preparation for the long, arduous migration to Africa. When the air becomes quiet after the birds have departed, I am bothered by the ensuing silence and it takes me a while to get used to relatively empty skies and the lack of activity, but at that moment it was alive with movement.

My client came out to greet me by my car with a worried expression. She asked me to follow her into a barn, where I assumed her horse would be. Instead, the woman led me to a pile of straw, and in a hollow I noticed a bird. Stopping to look more closely, I realised it was a young swallow. The woman explained that on arriving at the barn early that morning, she had noticed the fledgling on the ground, where he had either fallen from a nest, or, having landed, been unable to take off again. Adult birds had been swooping around the buildings, and, with the numerous swallow nests all now empty, the woman had considered where the young bird would be most safe and put him up onto a low, shady roof. She had hoped that he could take off from there or that a parent would attend to him. But as the sun had risen higher in the sky, the adult birds had gone further away from the buildings and so the woman had brought the fledgling into the cool barn. Could I give him healing and offer some advice as to what to do next?

Kneeling in the straw, I held my hands over the stricken swallow and could sense that he was very weak, with eyes shut and head lolling to one side. I felt that too many hours had passed by without the bird having fed (eating insects provides vital moisture too). An urgency possessed me to hold him in my hands and take him outside. It was an invitation that came from the bird, a need to be in an open space. Tenderly, I took the swallow into the scoop of my hands, noticing that he seemed almost weightless, and stepped out of the barn door to stand at the edge of a nearby field paddock and channel healing love to him.

I have worked with many injured wild creatures over the years, and therefore have some experience of how their energy feels whilst I am attempting to help them. As delicate as they are, birds have large, vibrant energy fields in relation to their size, and I could sense this little bird's energy system flowing within my hands. Above our heads the flock of swallows soared, swooped and communicated through a complex system of song, tweets, chirrups and telepathic messages. The numbers seemed to have increased since I had arrived and I noticed a group land on a telephone wire overhead, creating a chorus of noisy chattering before taking off in unison, flying into the distance, the first of this flock to begin the autumn migration. Ever higher into the sky they flew, calling to each other as they commenced their journey.

Suddenly the energy of the bird in my hands gathered into an intense volatile swirling mass – and I understood that he wanted to fly. What joy! I thought, the healing has worked its magic and he is going to be able to join his family after all. As I opened my hands, the bird stretched out his wings and flapped them vigorously for about fifteen seconds; every movement was that of flying, a surging momentum of soaring high and riding the thermals. His wing movements were not just up and down, but had a rapid rotational aspect too. It was awesome to witness close up this innate instinct to respond to the Earth's magnetic field and the air currents. The little fellow knew what he was doing all right, and was tuning into millions of years of bird knowledge. Here were a tiny heart and brain beating in my hands, a sort of 'all systems go' survival function kicking in, with full knowledge of what to do and why.

I admired the resplendent iridescent colours of his feathers, his small eye looking ahead, pointy beak, that pale splodge of red under the chin, soft white chest and the signature forked tail. He was so very beautiful that no artist could ever do him justice. Then there was a tumbling spin in my hands and the bird was lying on his back; the wing movements abruptly ceased. The bird had rolled over and passed away.

I was stunned, but information from the Healing Source quickly filtered into my mind, letting me understand what had occurred. The bird *had* flown; he had heeded the call of the flock to *'come join us'*. (It is known that when migrating birds gather they call to the young to fly with them, even if that means directly from the nest, a fraught time for late broods.) The bond with the flock had driven him to fulfil his life's purpose because he had been born to fly, and flown he had, first in my healer's hands then when his spirit swept high into the cosmos. The luminous feathered soul was merging with the world's birds and with the communal hub of Universal Energy that we all connect with. He flew with the migrating flock, supporting them as best he could, producing air currents from his ethereal wings, until he too reached home.

I am often reminded of the little bird in the breeze that wafts around my face, in the summer song of swallows or when I step into a barn and sense the history and knowledge left behind in an empty nest.

It is yet one more interaction imprinted in my heart and carved into my senses: a life lesson about fulfilling a sense of purpose, which applies to our own development as spiritual beings. One day, I hope to be as conscious and attentive as that little swallow to the fact that when something in our life has great meaning we don't give up. A sense of purpose is something that can inspire us to a great level of achievement and offers the potential for understanding the validity of other life forms. The little bird taught me that we are *all* important as part of the whole, for without us being here there are things that might not be accomplished.

Understanding our responsibility

Through increasing our understanding, we are urged to become responsible and consider the needs and behaviours of other species in our care, so that they have the freedom and choice to fulfil their own sense of purpose, or semblance of it. Shortly after the incident with the swallow, I found myself strolling through a town centre, thinking about the topic of freedom. Freedom means different things for each of us: the space to live without feeling cramped by neighbours; being able to make our own choices in everyday life; not feeling confined by a restrictive relationship; and being at liberty to live without restraint. And all these considerations equally apply to the needs of animals.

I was attending a conference at a university in an affluent north European city and, with a few hours spare, I wandered around the side streets. It was very hot for the time of year and as I turned a corner I noticed a café in a shady part of the street with several cloth-covered tables outside. The café looked cosy and inviting until I noticed a cage hanging from a window frame with a parrot inside it, perched on a pole.

Two pigeons were pecking underneath the parrot's cage at seeds that had dropped from it. One of the pigeons flew up to sit on the top of the cage and preened itself whilst the parrot tilted his head from side to side, looking up at the pigeon. Then both pigeons flew away, up over the rooftops, into the sunshine. Stepping forward, I held out my hands to the caged bird, offering healing, and at the same time asked, 'How does it feel not to have your freedom?'

The reply from the parrot came instantly: 'What is freedom?'

I understood from this exchange that the poor parrot was permanently incarcerated in the cage – just an ornament. The question 'What is freedom?' should never be asked of us by any creature. Our fellow Earth dwellers deserve far better, particularly now that science is increasingly confirming the extent of animal sentience.

Scientists speak out

Although animals and other creatures are restricted by lack of a verbal voice, scientists have discovered that animals can learn to use another human tool for communicating: pointing to symbols. Scientists are increasingly embracing the fact that animals are sentient in more ways than hitherto accepted, and some are calling for whales, dolphins and chimps to be given status as nonhuman persons. Even small animals like prairie voles have been proven to show altruistic behaviour. In fact, as I mentioned in the introduction, it's all too easy to forget that human beings are actually animals too, so maybe it should come as no surprise that science is providing more and more evidence that most animals are conscious in the same way that we are. Quite simply, the similarities between us are no longer something we can ignore.

In 2012, at the Francis Crick Memorial Conference in Cambridge, respected scientists declared that animals are so similar to human beings in terms of their consciousness and ability to think, feel and express emotions, they should be given similar rights as us. In January 2015, the French Parliament overturned 200 years of law to elevate animals to the status of sentient beings – 'not furniture' – and a little later in the year a court in New York declared chimps should have rights and status as nonhuman persons. In 2015, a bill in Quebec, Canada also ruled that animals have rights and are not property. New Zealand is acknowledging sentience in its own animal welfare legislation, and Holland has two members of parliament for animal rights. Similarly, several European countries have introduced legislation to help improve the lives of horses.

Although it seems obvious to most of us, this recognition in law represents an important milestone for animals. As the law begins to acknowledge the sentience of animals, acceptance will grow that animals have needs and desires of their own. Perhaps one day, animals globally will gain the rights that they have so long been denied.

Koko's bulletin

Koko is a great ape at the Gorilla Foundation who has been learning sign language since she was one year old. She was filmed delivering a bulletin for the 2016 International Climate Conference, in which she described how mankind is harming the Earth. In the minute-long video, the 44-year-old great ape said: 'I am gorilla, I am flowers, animals. I am Nature. Koko love man. Earth Koko love. But man stupid. Koko sorry, Koko cry. Fix Earth. Help Earth. Hurry. Protect Earth. Nature watches you. Thank you.'

It is a powerful message, and one that speaks volumes about our twenty-first-century attitudes. Thankfully, as an increasing number of world-renowned scientists talk about animals as nonhuman persons with thoughts, emotions and feelings that are similar to our own, accusations of being anthropomorphic are fast disappearing when it comes to animal communications. After all, nonhuman animals have been on this planet a great deal longer than the human species, and they could not have developed or survived without emotional intelligence and levels of innate, intuitive communication.

In his book *Are We Smart Enough to Know How Smart Animals Are?* Frans de Waal explores the scope and emotional depth of nonhuman animals and shows how the human species has grossly underestimated them. Ecologist Carl Safina, in his *New York Times* bestselling book *Beyond Words: What Animals Think and Feel*, mentions taking a risky step for a scientist:

> *I wanted to know what they were experiencing, and why to us they feel so compelling, and so close. This time I allowed myself to ask them the question that for a scientist was forbidden fruit: Who are you?*

It is a question that I too ask each and every animal that I meet, because the understanding that emanates from absorbing the information that comes my way paradoxically becomes who *I* am.

In his outstanding book *What a Fish Knows*, Jonathan Balcombe lifts the lid on the sentience of fish. We humans pride ourselves on complex social and cultural behaviours, but fish do all that stuff too. Given that fish are so like us – sentient, individual, social, intelligent and possessing a good sense of hearing – how can we treat them so badly? Commercial fishing continues to behave as though the oceans are infinite and now whole areas of ocean are effectively dead. One newspaper reviewer remarked on how we stagger around with bags of shopping destined ultimately for landfill or ocean-fill, firmly believing that it's the fish who are deaf. We need to listen harder to species in all the nooks and crannies.

Even plants possess an apparent sensitive cognizance. Peter Wohlleben's book *The Hidden Life of Trees* offers convincing evidence that trees have feelings too, and possess the ability to communicate, an example that can only encourage us to look even more deeply into animal consciousness.

In the face of all of this evidence, we face an urgent responsibility to establish the reality of the harm done through intensive agriculture, factory farming, certain methods of food production and the use of chemicals, puppy and kitten mills, abusive horse practices and the deprivation and misery of animals in captivity, including zoos and animal-entertainment theme parks. By making lifestyle adjustments we can all help.

When things get tough

Modern society is geared towards high achievers who are often very goal-oriented and can be quite hard on themselves. Sensitive people might find themselves overwhelmed by twenty-first-century life, but this in turn can lead to the realisation that it is not so much about learning how to function in the world and finding the holy grail of transferrable life skills than it is about actually perceiving and appreciating that there is a gentler way to live, through the unbiased friendship of animals.

When we are with animals we can learn by opening ourselves up to really *being* with that animal – how they think, feel and react to situations. We can ask what their world is like, how they see and sense the world. The nature of animals has helped me to better understand the diversity of the human condition. Having started out many years ago disillusioned by people and saying to myself 'I prefer animals to people', I have learnt from animals to have patience; otherwise we can't put into practice the lessons learnt from animals. We are each of us individual spiritual pilgrims seeking enlightenment through our experiences.

The human–animal bond can become a mutually dynamic and advantageous relationship that positively influences the health and wellbeing of both parties. While many of us intuitively understand the benefits of interactions with animals, research is increasingly highlighting the impact that the human–animal bond can have on both individual and community health. The mental, emotional and physical health of humans is inextricably linked to that of nonhuman animals; for example, recent research suggests that diseases affecting dolphins can serve as an early warning system about problems affecting human health.

We may find ourselves in life situations that cause us anguish and ask what we've done to deserve such treatment. There appears to be is no justice in the Universe, no reason for good people to suffer, and scant explanation or consolation for pain. At such times, animals – through their grace and generosity of spirit – can support us along our pathway through life.

Develop your level of understanding

Here are some simple practices to help deepen your own connection with animals and develop your understanding of the lessons they wish to share with you.

Check out places in your area where you can learn about animal behaviour.

Notice signs of the seasons and how this affects not just wild animals but domestic animals, including pets and horses.

Catch up on reading about animals and watch nature programmes on TV.

Listen to the 'teacher' sounds that animals direct to us. Tune into the complex range of vocal expressions that other beings use to exhibit signs of interaction, understanding and communication.

Change the way that you look at things by improving your focus and clarifying your thinking.

Celebrate the originality of animals, birds, insects and sea creatures. They illuminate and embellish the world.

Revealing your inner self

We often struggle to make sense of what is going on in our heads, and this exercise will help us to discover what we relate to and why. Try this game to reveal your inner mental and emotional compartments.

- Find a container of some sort: it could be a small box, plastic pot or large envelope, for example. If you wish, you can personalise the container by wrapping pretty paper around it. Tie or stick a label to your container and write your name on it.
- Over a few days, collect things from newspapers, magazines and other sources that 'speak' to you. If you live with an animal or animals, tune into them as you do this.
- Put the pieces that you collect into the container. Your scraps may include pictures or sections of them, words, phrases, notes that you jot down as random thoughts come to you, shapes or colours – in fact anything at all. You can also add small items that you find, such as leaves, petals, bark, seeds, shells, wood, stones or feathers.
- Don't analyse what you collect or think too much about it; instead, allow your mind to freewheel and your intuition to do the choosing, guided and inspired by your animal companions and contact with nature.
- After a week, or longer if you prefer, cease the collecting process and leave the container for a day or two. Now take each item out in the presence of your animal friend and consider what the fragments reveal about you. Why did you collect them?
- What appealed to you and how did the pieces relate to your thoughts, emotions and feelings at the time? Is there a pattern to your collection, in that they reveal a message that relates to the overall picture of what is going on in your life?

- Holding pieces from nature in your hands, and going into your place of inner stillness, will evoke their energy. This too can offer us information because the atoms in our bodies are the same as those in animals, plants, flowers, trees, even grass and in this way we possess a link.
- As you consider the objects, what do you sense the animal by your side is saying to you about your inner self? How does this improve your understanding of yourself and situations that you find yourself in?
- There is no right or wrong answer to this exercise, it is about revealing personal insights at that time.

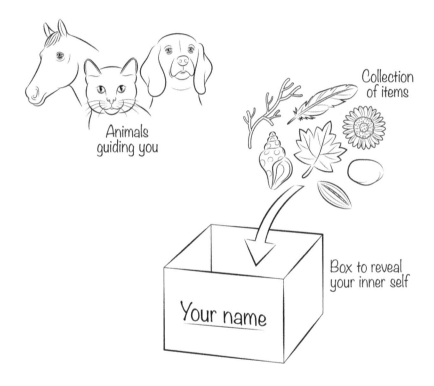

Animals guiding you

Collection of items

Box to reveal your inner self

Your name

I like to indulge in this exercise every few weeks, which often leads to inspiration regarding my projects and insights about everyday life. Some of the items that I have collected over the years I have placed into a heart-shaped basket as permanent reminders of progression through different times in my life.

Animals are highly aware of their surroundings. They can teach us to see the world differently. Animals possess a desire to understand their surroundings. Through association with them, their landscape of perception can seep into the fabric of our own sensory system

6. Shine

'And as we let our own light shine, we unconsciously give other people permission to do the same.'
Marianne Williamson

Animals offer us the perfect opportunity to leave our everyday stresses aside. With animals, we can drop our façade – the mask we put on each morning when we wake to face the day. Their company helps us to experience improved wellbeing and a fresh perspective. However, animals see beyond our veneer when they look at us: they assess how much light we are emitting. As I indicated in the chapter 'Open Your Heart', time and again, animals communicate to me that they check humans out in terms of how much light we radiate from our inner selves, seeing it like a star at our core. Just like sound is a wavelength, another of the energy wavelengths in a body is light; and the level of our inner luminosity is an indicator of several things to animals, including our health, mood, thoughts, compassion and empathy. Our radiating light also contains the history of who we are and what we have done. The more elevated our altruism towards all forms of life, the brighter we shine. We humans often have difficulty sensing this light in others until we begin to listen to our intuition; then we can detect the energy, which will in turn help us assess who is literally on our wavelength.

I often meet people who tell me they've been to an animal shelter with the intention of taking home a particular type of dog or cat, yet they returned with something very different instead, because a particular animal reached out to them soul to soul. Frequently during consultations, I've heard horse owners say things such as, 'I went to a dealer to get a brown gelding and I came home with a black mare – and I don't know why, but I just had to do it!' Through my own experiences with animals, I have an inkling why this happens. The animals were attracted to the light transmitting from those individuals, which shone more brightly in relation to other people in the vicinity. In such situations, animals send out messages such as, 'Please take me home with you,' which we are able to hear and respond to on a soul level.

Having had conversations with animals for many years about their ability to see light energy in all life forms (not just humans), I was delighted when something concrete happened to prove that we do indeed emit light – and that this light plays a role in the phenomenon of healing energy.

Light display

It was early January and I had travelled down to Devon to teach for the day. The weather was fairly typical for the time of year, cold with a wintry light-grey sky, but thankfully in view of my long drive, snow had not yet arrived. It was close on my heels, though, with a telltale icy blast in the air as I walked amongst the horses. I had asked for the artificial lights to be turned off in the barn because I prefer to work in natural light when possible. Openings in the outer barn walls let in the daylight, which softly diffused the area where I was working. It was not bright, but it was peaceful.

The organiser of the day asked if she could take some photos and I noticed that she had a good-quality camera. Stepping into the middle of barn, I touched the first horse and started to discuss the benefits of healing energy. The organiser duly pointed her camera and started clicking away, but after a couple of minutes she asked me to stop, citing a problem.

'There's something weird going on,' she said. 'Come and look at this.'

When she reviewed the first couple of photos that she had taken of me working with the horse, she'd noticed a pale splodge on the image. The woman assumed there was something on the lens, a fingerprint or dust perhaps, so she cleaned the lens with a special cloth from her camera bag. When the next image still contained the mark, the woman changed camera angle several times, yet the strange splodge remained. Even when she zoomed in to take a photo, the image contained the shadowy mark.

What I saw took my breath away: a set of pictures in which there was a whitish tube coming from the middle of my body and connecting me to the horse. It was a tube of light. Because the photographer had taken so many varied angles we had evidence that the light was not on the lens, because it was in a different position on each image. The light clearly connected with the core of my body just above my waist.

Nevertheless, we checked the inside of the barn just in case any light was trickling in from another external source, but there was none, and if there had been it would have appeared on the same place in all the photos. The position of the tube-like light in these photographs wasn't static, although it was uniform in shape.

There seemed to me to be no explanation other than that it was a gift from the Universe to show me that what the animals had told me was true. I have no idea how this lesson came to manifest itself in this way for me and others to see, but I am very grateful that it did. Through time spent with animals, I have learnt that you can't ask for signs, yet every now and again evidence appears. And it is truly fascinating to gather together these pieces of knowledge.

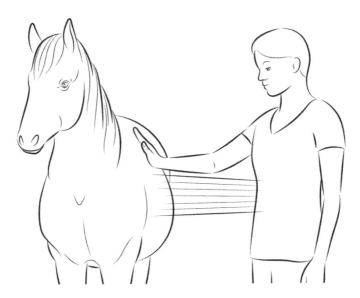

This illustration shows what animals can see – a light that connects us to other beings. This can be strong or weak, bright or dull depending on how we are feeling, our thoughts, intentions, actions and the depth of our unconditional love. When we approach animals as equal souls, our light glitters and sparkles, attracting them to us

> Animals reflect light into our hearts helping us feel carefree and happy during our days, and this is why we need them in our lives. And we can also pass on this gift of light from animals to others, in a never-ending circle of radiance.

Sparkle

There are days when I despair at the increasing turmoil in the world. One morning, after watching worrying news on TV, I logged on to my laptop and Leonard Cohen's song 'Anthem' jumped out at me, which mentions that in everything there is a crack through which light seeps in.

As I mulled over the succinct phrase, one of my cats leapt onto my lap with a *prrrp* noise to rub my face in greeting, and I was delightfully reminded that animals are wonderful experts at shining light into human hearts to help us sparkle.

Because our light can be dimmed through circumstances, including relationships, work or illness, it is important to do something each day to keep it shining brightly. Our soul clarity and our radiance are both boosted by being with animals and in nature.

I love my work with animals because it means I meet a lot of different characters during my teaching and my consultations. Whenever they appear, a smile beams across my face and I am filled with anticipation and excitement; and I want to go and introduce myself if possible. This is something that also happens when I am out and about: in a crowded shopping mall, for instance, I might look down and notice a dog's nose peeping from behind a human leg; or when I am in town I might see a dog bounding along in a park at the end of a leash. My urge to say hello to the dog often leads to conversations with people that would not otherwise have taken place. We take our leave smiling, and the day feels much brighter. When I meet cats in the streets I talk to them too, although their humans are not usually around, and I make a beeline to chat to horses wherever I find them. It is the soul light in animals that is so attractive to me.

Dogs are amazing, playful teachers

During my pet events, the room lights up when the real teachers come in – the dogs. The dogs who attend these events love being enthusiastically greeted; their lessons are going to be vitally important that day and they seem to know it. We can't have cats present at these events unfortunately, because generally they are not as used to going to different places and situations as dogs are, but like dogs they are amazing teachers. Horses are so good at teaching humans about themselves and triggering life improvements that they are frequently included in therapy sessions for a wide range of situations, as well as being involved in business coaching.

All of these master teachers are wonderful at keeping me on my toes and helping me evaluate my learning. Animals are fun to be with and can make us laugh, the best medicine. No wonder connecting with them is so rewarding, as their company can teach us how to truly shine.

Looking up some meanings of 'shine' and 'light', I came across these related phrases:

Look on the bright side; shine a light; seeing the light; guiding light; eyes shining; stand out and shine …

We can choose any one of these terms and focus on it as an area for personal development.

The complexities of life can sometimes leave us feeling stressed out and depleted. Through reminding ourselves that there are two things that we can control or choose – our thoughts and our actions – animals guide us further along the path of miracles by encouraging us to explore ourselves as soul beings. The soul thrives in the light; and the light allows our natural talents to shine through.

In our face

Every now and then, somebody will attend one of my workshops or a consultation looking troubled. They may have personal problems or a sick animal at home, or have recently said goodbye to a soul mate. As time passes, however, there is often a noticeable shift in these people's expressions as they move towards a deeper awareness of animals, thereby drawing closer to them. As we plumb the meaning of how and why animals give us so much, and we draw mentally and emotionally closer to those creatures present with us, the atmosphere changes. It becomes ethereal and almost fluorescent in texture. In these situations you can actually see the brightness suffuse people's faces, and I particularly enjoy that moment when a troubled demeanour starts to slide away – like the moment at dawn when the first rays of light spread out into the nooks and crannies of dark corners.

'You're shining, your face looks like sunshine!' is something I love being able to tell people. It brings a whole new meaning to the concept of the light dawning on us. And animals approve of this happiness because it has a knock-on effect generally in our everyday lives: our sparkly demeanour is attractive to others, meaning that our relationships flow more easily. Perhaps without our even realising it, our good humour brightens the energy of others as well, thereby helping them feel uplifted. Through the sensitivity of animals, I am often reminded that light attracts light, and until we let go of our ridiculous assumption that we are superior and more sentient than our fellow beings on this planet, we will find ourselves struggling in the dark.

Enrichment of our lives occurs when we let the light shine.

Letting the light shine, feline style.
To receive it, we just have to listen to them

Creative synergy

An approach to life that fosters a close sense of connection with all beings is more popular today than ever before, across all levels of society, in various guises. Art, music, creative writing and gentle relaxation exercises can all play a part in this kind of approach.

Animals can also act creatively, aware of the potential outcomes of their actions; research has shown that their behaviour is not just determined by their intuitive responses. A few examples of this include chimps making spears from sticks, crows crafting leaves, twigs and feathers into tools, elephants using rocks to short out electric fences, sea otters breaking open clams with stones and octopuses adapting discarded coconut shells to make a shelter. Other species' innovation is of course different from ours, but there is a synergy about it, and animals can help us express ourselves so that we shine creatively too.

Anyone can create art either by drawing or writing, and in this way we can make our mark, not just on paper, but in terms of exploring who we are. As a child I kept a scrapbook in which I noted what garden birds were doing, and it was the start of my passion for recording and honouring the life about me. Activities such as scrapbooking have a minimal financial outlay and are an easy way to cultivate the spiritual talents that might be lying dormant within us.

Creativity works to improve our mindset. A US study found that when students were given a list of words to recall, they were able to correctly remember twice as many when they drew pictures of them, compared with simply writing down the words. Apparently drawing integrates several brain processes, which helps create a more cohesive memory; so if we draw pictures relating to animals then it could be that we will better integrate with their world.

Human disconnection from nature is one of the biggest issues on the planet today, yet a fulfilling connection with nature will enhance our lives to the point where this changes who we are. We can move away from stormy thoughts and begin to spiritually shine. This elevated state of mind, which can be referred to as mindfulness, connects us to our potential for inner healing.

As an adult, I have continued my habit of writing in notebooks – jotting down the things I sense or feel, the details of the animals I meet and of natural events, as well as, of course, the inspired thoughts that enter my mind through my connection with animals. I keep a soul diary, and if I am seeking an answer to something but am not sure how to go about it, or am seeking guidance in a situation, I often find the solution pops into my mind – almost like a mushroom growing from nowhere. It can also feel like there is an inner voice giving me the information I need, and I now know this voice to be the Universal hub of knowledge infusing me with what I should pay attention to. It is a lovely warm feeling when that happens, and I make sure to write down what I've learnt. I sometimes describe my notebook as being like a cake in which the ingredients are words, drawings, descriptions, annotations, ideas and thoughts. They are what I experience, see, think and feel as I share my life with animals.

A very special entry in my notebook records the sound I heard when I was in British Columbia, Canada. I was woken by a sound stirring my soul – a primeval noise that reverberated through the night. Wolves calling! The sound echoed across the valley from somewhere on the next mountain, and in my mind's eye I 'saw' the lifted necks, the open jaws, the breath moving through the vocal chords to form the unmistaken utterances of the wolf. The voice of the wolf.

A majestic scene lay beyond my bedroom window – a full moon, silvery in a deep-grey sky; pale clouds framing the black outlines of fir trees scattered down the valley slopes. There was no wind to disturb the air, just the sound of wolves baying. The romantic in me likes to think that they were perhaps singing to the moon, and for that reason I bought a painting of a howling wolf as a reminder of my trip before returning home. After a couple of minutes the wolf song faded and I went back to bed, wondering if I would ever see a wild wolf close up. The Universe, it turned out, was listening to my wish, because some time later I had my incredible encounter with the timber wolf I mentioned earlier.

Shine a poem

Wherever I am, walking under trees, across fields or beside water, I can feel the way animals connect to everything, and I too am drawn into this – and remember that I am part of everything. It's like simultaneously growing roots and having wings.

Every day I have to get out of the house, take a walk, and look at all the animals in the countryside around me – the rabbits, deer and birds. Then I realise that they are all individuals whose life is as important to them as mine is to me. I can hear them speaking to me and each other, their voices radiating far away into the distance. They are not voices like my own, but a transmission of waves of energy that are full of information. In this state, I find that I have a heightened awareness, and when I return home I feel replenished. My mind contains inspired thoughts or images that I then take time to record in my soul diary.

Contact with nature and animals brings out the poet in us – and you too possess this potential. Animals can communicate information to us through their soul voice, and when we write this down it can create a poetic message. You may now be thinking, 'Oh, I can't possibly do that, poetry's about making words rhyme,' but it's actually an easier creative process than that, which each person can achieve.

Animals, birds and sea creatures resonate with lyrical insights, influencing our senses whenever we are in their proximity. They can all bring out the poetry within us, which is part of the ballad of our shining light.

Release your inner poet

This is how you can start to access your inner poet: simply be with your animals or wander about outside in a place in nature that you like.

Take a notebook with you and jot down whatever words come to you, no matter how obvious they seem. Looking at your animal friend, you may feel inspired to write something like 'soft, brown and furry, bright eyes, pointy ears'; looking at the sky, maybe you write 'blue, birds flying' or 'pale and cloudy'; or, on spotting a flower, simply 'petals, leaves, stalk'.

All around us are creatures living in their own worlds, yet moving simultaneously through ours. As you take your walk, know that you are striding alongside the parallel worlds of other beings.

Transmit some questions to the animals or birds around you. Through being in your place of inner stillness, see what answers reverberate back to you. What insights do you receive? What animal voices do you hear? How are you inspired?

There is no right or wrong, it is all OK. If, at first, you find the words don't come easily, choose some familiar phrases that you like and jot them down to get yourself started. When the words begin to flow, just add more until you find you have some sentences.

Whenever I do this exercise and read back what I have written, I am often amazed at how the meaning jumps out at me, which is frequently related to things going on in my life at the time.

Creating together

Another useful exercise involves getting together with several like-minded people. First, arrange to meet up again with the group at an appointed time. Then, in silence, go your own ways. Tune into any animals that are present, or go for a walk outside, making notes of any words or sentences inspired by animal wisdom.

When the group meets up again, each person selects a single sentence from their notes that describes an encounter with an animal or with nature that day, and writes this down on a strip of paper. All the strips are then collected in a small box.

The box is passed around, with each person randomly taking out a note. Each note is now numbered (the first piece of paper picked out becomes number 1 and so on). Finally, someone reads the words on the pieces of paper in the order in which they were selected.

The poetry that emanates can be amazing and it's always a lot of fun. Remember that poetry does not need to rhyme; it is about the meaning and beauty of language.

Once you have assembled the poem with your friends, you can discuss the meaning in each sentence, as well as the message in the poem as a whole. You might find it helpful to think about how that message relates to your life at this time.

Three wonderful poems

During one retreat that I taught on a mountain in North America, the participants came up with the incredible poem below – the result of their spending several hours communing with the land, trees, plants, birds, mountains, lake, deer, squirrels, horses, dogs, cat and pet steer. Reading out the collective message after it had been collated gave us all goose bumps. Each person's voice is unique and there is no greater or lesser line; everything in the message is equal and valuable. I have left in the names of those who took part to show how this exercise works.

The stars are out, big and bright, shining down on Earth tonight (Kit)

Let the sound be your guiding light (Tamara)

Inner stillness prompts deeper listening (Jonathan)

The land is bursting with beautiful energy (Peter)

We are bonded forever no matter where we are (Wendy)

The essence of your pure heart is all you require (Karen)

I feel at peace and am deeply grateful to all the contributors to my healing (Michelle)

Dare to feel again, feel deeper and deeper, open your heart and become one with all there is (Petra)

Remember to count the stars one by one; it is not getting it done but the joy along the way that matters (Barbara)

Come dance with us within the pause (Marianne)

When you spend time in the quiet, sincerely in search of truth you will find it; you will remember it for it is there in your soul (Liz)

Deep down in the cracked ancient log, pony and I are one with the Ant nation (Elizabeth)

Breath in the lands, whisper your truth (Kevin)

Around every corner there are surprises, as the old reveals the new (Margrit)

Fluid, shifting, changing, glorious peace (Julie)

Blossom of love, may you bloom and grow (Connie)

The roller-coaster ride of life reveals a timeless source of peace (Rebecca)

Nature's beauty transforms the human spirit and always moves us closer towards love and light (Rhyan)

This is a profound message from a group of people at Mane Chance Horse Sanctuary in the UK, inspired by their horses:

You're all right
Continue
Healing is your path
Do what you can
Harmonise
Love me, don't be afraid

Believe in yourself
Let the light shine
Trust your own healing power
Use kindness and love
It's time to speak out
Thank you, I love you
Happy and Healing
Let's help each other

And here is a group poem from a pet workshop in the Netherlands:

Look around, don't overlook the peace
Where are you, just be there
We are all connected
The soul can travel far
You are so beautiful, can't you see
Let me show you what unconditional love is all about
Peace
Just be, that's all you need to do
You don't need the drama
Beauty is on the inside
Relax into the silence and surrender into the deep unknown
Thank you for caring unconditionally
Consciousness on Earth
Trust yourself and your intuition
See yourself through my eyes
Stay curious, and there is the possibility to learn
What you do to me, you do to yourself

It intrigues me how, each time I do this exercise, the bias is slightly different in the message that animals have conveyed to the group. Yet it never fails to astound me how the collective message always relates to a particular theme that is helpful to the group as a whole. More often than not, the message relates to the world situation as well as to our individual lives, as though the animals know the state of global affairs (which, of course, they do!) and wish to help us understand things beyond our control. Animals want to help us – and this exercise is an easy way to access their guidance.

Animals lead us to beauty

Art and soul

Sadly, formal art teaching can sometimes close us off, leading us to think that we have not painted or drawn something in the 'right' way, which belies our true healing nature. For our Higher Self is artistic and creative. All we need to do to get started is to place the tip of a pencil onto a piece of paper and then allow our hand to move. It's that easy! After all, even complex famous pieces of artwork are just a combination of marks: dots, dashes, lines, squiggles, blobs and smudges.

Here is a very simple way to help expand your creativity: all you have to do is to write down the words of a poem on a sheet of paper and then add colours, shapes and images to it – or even make the whole thing into a poster. Explore any ideas as they come to you.

You could also take your art materials and sit with an animal outdoors, either in a garden or in nature. Tune into the animal, mind to mind, using your intuition. Now draw whatever you sense that the animal is focusing on, and how he or she perceives it in terms of shape, texture and colours. In this way you can develop a psychic level of artistry.

As you will soon discover if you venture outdoors, creatures in the wild don't pose; they might only be glimpsed for an instant, but in that time we can often capture the essence of the animal or bird – the shape of an ear, a tail moving, a wing swishing. Other things remain static for our consideration: a tree, plant, cloud or pond, for example, all offer visual opportunities to stimulate our consciousness. These things can evolve into beautiful images when translated onto paper, either in words or marks. Simplicity often becomes the most stunning creation.

The leaf art here was created by a veterinarian during one of my retreats. Having chosen a leaf as inspiration, she drew simple shapes of a kind that really anyone can manage – and the patterned result, I'm sure you will agree, is lovely.

Giving a piece of your peace

When you have made several marks and art images in your own soul diary, in which you can also record moments of inspiration, consider passing on a piece of your peace. This is how to do it.

Copy your marks onto a blank card using a soft pencil. You can do this randomly or in a pattern. Then take some coloured pens and go over the marks as you feel inspired. You can stick on coloured pieces of paper, glitter, or small pieces of fabric, in whatever way you feel represents the connection you had to the animals when you made notes in your mindfulness record.

Then send or give the card to someone whose day will be brightened as a result. You have given a gift of your peace.

Letting it flow

New names for art pastimes come and go, and the scribblings with which I filled my notebooks as a child was called doodling. Yet when I developed this practice during my art-college training, it was described as abstract drawing.

For me, drawing has always been a way to release tension and express creativity, as well as to unpack ideas and find solutions to problems. Over the years, I have often enjoyed exploring my connection to animals and nature by expressing myself creatively, letting images flow and evolve as though they are using my hands to record themselves in the form of my artistic representations.

This sort of creative flow is quite Zen-like, yet easy to achieve and involves little expenditure, apart from investing in some paper and pencils/pens. Or, if you want to go digital, tablets have drawing apps that can be downloaded and used to good effect for your own Animal Zen Doodling.

Animal Zen Doodle

This is my version of doodling with a Zen slant. I've found it to be a useful way to tune into the guidance of animals, with all the benefits this can bring. The rewards of this exercise lie not only in the resulting piece of art but in the process: you may find your mind detangles as you create your own Animal Zen Doodle and your mood is lifted. The Universe is always listening to our thoughts, emotions and feelings and you may be surprised at how, once you begin your doodle, the process seems to take over and guide your hand.

Take a blank sheet of paper and divide it into six to nine squares. Watch an animal (you may be with the animal in person, or perhaps looking through a window at a scene). Make a representation of the animal in one of the squares. Don't hold back, or feel intimidated – you are not competing with Rembrandt! This is an expression of your own uniqueness.

Now consider how the animal might feel to your touch, or bring to mind actual memories of touching it, and represent this sensation in another of the squares. Squiggles, lines, shapes are all valid – this is about your expression in relation to your personal experiences.

Next, move on to another square and think about the colours of the animal, and his or her texture, such as the hair/fur/feathers/skin. Make your marks here through a reflection of what it means to you. This is calming in itself.

Animals are masters of movement in complex ways. Fill in a square with some lines representing the dynamics of animal activity, exertion and progression. Reflect on how noting the motion helps you move away from tension.

Animals have wonderful ways of expressing themselves, so here is where you can fill a square with something that you find particularly attractive about them. The look in an eye, a tail wagging, a smile, for example.

Let the creative juices flow until you have filled all of your squares. Take your time, don't rush; the more you focus on different aspects of your animal or nature topic, the easier it is to relax.

You can either leave the drawing as pen or pencil, or colour in the sections. Be creative with your choice of hues and tones; this is about the expression of you.

It is useful to repeat this exercise often and see how your collection of drawings expands and maps the theme of your life lessons. Most importantly, have fun while you do your doodling – fun being something that animals always encourage. Keep your Animal Zen Doodles in a special folder for future reference. If you have a favourite, it can even be framed and hung on a wall as a special memento of your life with animals.

Movements the dog makes. Feel this awareness set you free to expore life.

Colours radiating into your psyche

You recall the dog's eye, the way it speaks to you, the loving expression.

Places you have been with the dog, walks, things you saw, where you stopped. Memories!

Here you draw the animal you have chosen to Zen Doodle.

Thinking about your experiences of touching a dog. You express them here: soft, warm, smooth, rough, healing.

Example of an Animal Zen Doodle assisted by a dog (although you can do this exercise with any animal).

It's personal

I've said it before, and I'll say it again: everyone can create something artistic. But if you initially lack confidence in this area, I suggest you keep your efforts for your eyes only at first. The knowledge that our notes and drawings are personal and not for anyone else's scrutiny allows freedom of expression. If you like what you create, that's all that matters – because animals encourage us to believe in our abilities. They don't judge our creative process from an ego perspective or with envy; they appreciate whatever makes us happy. When we continually compare ourselves to others, we miss out on developing our potential. Critical comments can destroy self-expression, when what we need instead is to respect how and what we each create.

Art is primarily about making a mark, yet it is symbolic too. It is an expression of who we are. And the most creative work that any of us can accomplish is ourselves.

Animals guide us to become our own masterpiece.

7. Play

'This is the real secret of life – to be completely engaged with what you are doing in the here and now. And instead of calling it work, realise it is play.'

Alan W. Watts

I love to play with animals. Then I can be like a child again – giggle and laugh, shout with joy and fling myself around with abandon, unconcerned about achieving anything other than playing. We need to remember to play. Through play, animals encourage us to be active and explore our surroundings, teaching us about movement and exercise. This not only improves our overall sense of wellbeing but our ability to learn. In animals, play leads to higher intelligence, innovation and increased flexibility. The smarter the animals, the more that they want to play. And humans are ingenious, right? But we often forget how to be playful in a therapeutic, non-destructive way. And unfortunately humans can ignore or misinterpret invitation-to-play signals from animals, leading to misunderstanding on both sides.

In the animal kingdom, playful animals may invite potential aggressors to join in and become friends, in the way that film footage has shown huskies playing with polar bears. Play, and implementing love and respect towards the world's animals, has a knock-on beneficial effect on relationships that we have with others. Play can also be a form of experiential exploration or research.

In the animal kingdom play forms an essential part of forging friendships. When we interact playfully with the animals in our lives, this helps deepen our mutual respect as well as improve the level of communication between us. Scientists have produced evidence that a sense of humour isn't exclusive to humans and we can find proof of this in a wide variety of animal species. In experiments at Bowling Green University in Ohio, USA, rats have been observed making ultra-sonic chirps of pleasure when play-fighting and playing chase, and making the same sounds when being tickled. It seems to be their signal of laughter.

A series of uplifting photographs showing an orangutan's reaction to a conjuring trick has been circulated around the world. The images showed a researcher performing a sleight-of-hand trick with a cup and a chestnut; first the person showed the animal a chestnut in the cup and then secretly removed it before again showing the cup. At first the orangutan was puzzled by the 'now you see it, now you don't' phenomenon, but then it dawned on him what was going on and he responded by rolling on the floor in what we would describe as a glorious fit of hilarity.

Interaction with my cat and dog pals has shown me that they too have a sense of humour. My cat Teddy liked to play hide and seek in the garden with his sister Lilly, darting out from the depths of a shrub as she walked past. She would of course sense that he was there, halting in a game of stalemate. But Teddy would still ambush her in a cat version of *Boo,* sending Lilly leaping into the air.

To amuse herself, my Sheltie friend Gina has created a trick whereby whilst other dogs are lined up in front of me on the beach to intently watch a ball in my hand, she sneaks behind them and stares at a tail. As soon as I throw the ball and the dogs run off after it, Gina grabs that particular tail and momentarily holds the other dog back before letting go. Gina completes the game by running around in circles barking, full of glee as though she is shouting, 'Ha ha, got you!'

Through similar anecdotes of our own, we can therefore understand that animals appreciating comedy as part of play isn't as far-fetched as it sounds, and is something that, through animal encounters, we can come across on a regular basis. It's not just humans who can see a joke.

Fun is contagious

I've experienced some of my happiest moments through meetings with remarkable animals. There was the time when I was visiting New Zealand,

and whilst sitting by the sea, heard loud voices coming from people in a small boat close to the shore. The reason for their excitement was that a dolphin had jumped out of the sea, over their boat. Suddenly the incoming waves became alive with the dark shapes of dolphins surfing side by side, before leaping and spinning up into the air. The sea bubbled; the dolphins seemed to be everywhere, swimming around or flipping upwards, out of the water, before splashing down again. A local man came over to talk to the watching crowd and explained that the spectacle involved a pod of Dusky dolphins.

For the next hour we watched the dolphins play. They jumped over waves and into waves; they rode the waves like body-board surfers; they splashed close to boats; and when you got a glimpse of their faces, you could see they were having a fun time. Best of all for me was the fact that we were being entertained by these intelligent beings in their natural element, not as captive slaves in a marine park forced to do tricks for a meal. The dolphins were family and friends and to watch them play without restraint was fascinating and humbling.

After a while I wondered why my face was aching and then I realised it was because I had been smiling for the whole time that the dolphins swam before us. It was the highlight of our holiday. In my mind I can still see the frolicking quite clearly, and my heart will always remember the dolphins rejoicing in the sea.

More recently, some friends took me to visit the pioneering Durrell Wildlife Conservation Trust, and the first thing we went to see was a group of golden lion tamarin monkeys. The mammal expert accompanying us called out to the monkeys and they came over, running along a network of ropes and trees to reach us. A small human-like face appeared in a bush in front of me, and then the head rotated as the animal hung by his tail and reached forward to take the grape that I was offering. Three more monkeys moved forward, each carefully touching my hand to draw a grape towards them, before bouncing away to sit and munch on the fruit. Somewhere nearby a child was shouting and creating a hubbub, and I looked around to see who had invaded our privacy at this precious moment. Only my friends and the conservation guide stood there. The noise was coming from me: the evergreen child inside me was merrily yelling its head off – the sense of playful joy was fabulously contagious!

I was then taken to the bat house, a world-renowned centre of excellence which supports critically endangered fruit bats. After being with the frolicking monkeys it was like walking into a library from a school playground, such was the pervading atmosphere of 'hush'. Groups of bats hung upside down watching me. Livingstone's fruit bats are a huge species with beautiful, inquisitive, bear-like faces, and as with the monkeys (and indeed all animals that I meet) there was a rapidly unfolding sense of being greeted by a group of individual personalities who were all sussing me out. Laughter was bubbling up inside me, but I kept it from bursting out of my mouth, not wanting to alarm the bats, instead letting it seep out of the pores of my skin. Someone took hold of my hand and, turning, I met the gaze of a bat who had moved very close to me. Bats have a thumb situated at the leading edge of their wings, which has a substantial claw. It was this that had been hooked around my finger by the bat. *'Could I please have that tasty piece of banana that you are holding?'* was the evident message. The bat quickly began eating it, accompanied by lip-smacking noises of pleasure. Then more bats ventured forward and I found myself in the midst of their curiosity and friendship. Some days are glorious fun and this was one of those times.

The cat that came to play

Animals clearly have the ability to help us play and frolic, which are good for our health and wellbeing. Here is an example of how an animal can help us find equilibrium when we feel troubled.

Sheila and Don had downsized after thirty-seven years in their much loved home. It had been hard to sort out their belongings, especially when it came to giving away possessions, as the new place was much smaller than the house they were leaving. Each item had a story attached to it, and Sheila in particular found herself reliving the past as she handled the bits and pieces. Every open drawer or cupboard was full of complex memories. In this house they had raised their son, tragically taken from them as a teenager through an accident.

The new property was located in a more densely populated neighbourhood and the couple struggled to get used to the change. A few months after the move, just as late autumn pointed her icy fingers towards the town, Sheila went into their new garden to fill up the bird feeders. A movement on a wall by her shoulder caught her attention and, turning, she found herself eye to eye with a ginger tom. The cat rubbed his head along the edge of the wall, appeasement language for *I want to be your friend, please like me.*

'You're pretty,' Sheila said to the cat. 'Where have you come from?' In reply, the cat promptly jumped down the other side of the wall and disappeared.

The tom returned most days after that to watch Sheila and Don pottering about in their garden. Because he looked rather unkempt, the couple suspected their feline visitor might be a stray. Several weeks later, as heavy rain set in, the cat appeared by their back door just as the couple were carrying in bags of shopping from the car. Creeping past them into the kitchen, he huddled by the warmth of a log-burning stove.

Although never having lived with a pet before, Sheila and Don immediately agreed they liked the company of their animal visitor and let the cat stay a while. When they noticed him twitch his nose as their fish supper was cooked, the cat was offered some. When bedtime came Don left a small window open so that their feline guest could leave when he was ready, and they didn't expect to see him in the morning. But the next day, they found the cat in the same place, stretched out on a mat in the warmth. As they ate their breakfast, watching the cat play with a piece of string snaffled from inside a box, the couple commented how he seemed to have made himself at home and that the atmosphere of the room felt different. It was filled with something they could not quite put their finger on. It was even, said Don, laughing at the play antics, as if the cat had always been with them.

All the same, later that day Don called some animal shelters to see if a ginger cat had been reported missing, but drew a blank. One of the shelters told the couple to take the cat to a vet to see if there was a microchip, but when they did none was discovered. The vet estimated the cat's age to be around two. Ginger, as he was then named, now had a home.

Several years later, I was called in to offer some healing help after Don had suddenly passed away, leaving both Sheila and Ginger bereft. Ginger had grown particularly close to Don after his adoption by the couple and loved to spend his evenings sitting on the man's lap, eyes closed and purring softly. Sheila mentioned to me that Ginger's arrival had resulted in her husband becoming more contented and less irritable, and his depression had lifted. The couple had both joined the local tennis club and also taken to walking a neighbour's dog.

I asked Sheila why she thought these changes had come about, and, mulling the question over for a minute, she replied: 'Somehow Ginger's playful character brought a vitality which made the atmosphere feel welcoming for us. It not only lifted our mood but motivated Don to become more active in his own life. The house took on a bright energy, where before it seemed empty even though we were living here. We found friendship in each other again and both became more active. Now I'm glad that I have Ginger by my side to help me with the loss of my husband; I'm not alone.'

Sheila showed me some photos of them both with Ginger, and reminisced about the games they had played together. Ginger's favourites were when they spread a sheet of tissue paper over a pile of leaves, which resulted in an exciting jump and rummage, or chasing a stick with a piece of string dangling from it. It was exciting play for Ginger and hilarious for Sheila and Don to watch, just going to show the many different ways in which animals can provide companionship, offer fun times and stimulate us out of stagnation.

A cat's curiosity will express itself in play

Clever dogs

Leo and Moo are mostly very contented Labradors, especially as their owners, Rachel and James, make sure daily to join in with their favourite games, helping to strengthen their relationship with the dogs. It was only because of some niggling health problems that I was brought in to help. Whenever I visit, Moo greets me with a toothy smile, upper lip curled back to reveal gleaming teeth, whilst bouncing on the spot as though he wants to leap into my arms, whereas Leo usually appears with a favourite toy hanging from his mouth, his eyes doing the smiling. Then we invariably have a game in the garden of 'throw the ball' before settling down to the serious business of me tuning into them and offering healing.

One day, I was sitting on the floor with my hands on Moo, and chatting to Rachel about the ageing process that we all suffer from. After a pause Moo suddenly communicated to me that he knew he was a middle-aged dog but that play motivated him to feel young at heart. An image then ballooned into my consciousness, transmitted from Moo's mind. As I started to describe this scene to Rachel, more and more details emerged, as though I was not to miss anything out. I was shown a palette of colours forming a sweep of unspoilt beach; to the right of the beach a jumble of rocks spilled along a peninsula and there was an upland of mountains in the distance. This was, Moo informed me, his favourite place to play.

Rachel was intrigued and, switching on her laptop, started to scroll through photos of a place in Scotland that she, her husband and the dogs were soon to revisit. She asked if anything fitted the description. One of the photos was identical to Moo's disclosure. As soon as I identified it, Moo jumped up and nudged the laptop as a mark of affirmation, his trademark toothy grin reinforcing his pleasure that his message had been heard. We told Moo how clever he was and thanked him for sharing one of his secrets with us.

During their subsequent Scottish holiday, Rachel and James visited an art gallery and chose two paintings to be sent to their home. One painting depicted Moo's favourite cove, and the other was of the sea lit up in shades of red and orange by a spectacular sunset. When the two packages were opened, Moo and Leo ignored the sea scene, but were clearly fascinated by the painting of the beach – so much so that they sniffed it, tried to paw at it and even to lick it, which was unusual behaviour for them with regard to new household items. When Rachel hung the picture on the wall, the dogs lay side by side, staring up at it like visitors in a studio admiring the work of a favourite artist. Eventually the dogs stretched out and fell asleep, I believe to dream of holiday bliss and fun times.

Leo is a thoughtful observer and was no doubt aware that Moo received heaps of praise for his revelation about the holiday destination. It was as though he had bided his time to trump Moo's confession, because shortly afterwards he communicated that he was going to spill the beans about something that had happened. Turning to Rachel, I asked her if she wanted me to continue – just in case it might have been something rather embarrassing. Leo's gentle gaze flicked across to Rachel, who became caught up in the amusing atmosphere and encouraged him to continue. *'There has been an argument,'* I heard Leo say, *'with raised voices!'* – and this had worried him. As I passed this message on to Rachel, Moo immediately looked anxious and rushed over to stare at Leo, as if to say, *'Should you be spilling the beans about this?'*

Rachel was quick to establish the ins and outs of Leo's revelation. A difference in opinion had led Rachel and James to have, unusually for them, a robust conversation. She was able to reassure Leo that the matter was now fully resolved and the harmony that they were used to was completely restored. Leo responded by rolling over onto his back with a happy sigh.

That evening, when James came home from work, Rachel started to recount what had occurred during my visit. Now it was Leo's turn to act in an anxious manner, throwing himself across Rachel's lap as if to say, *'I wish I hadn't said anything, I'm so embarrassed about it.'* Leo was reassured that it was fine to communicate whatever he wanted to and not to worry about doing so, because he too was a clever boy. Leo then ran to fetch his favourite toy and asked for a game.

The expression says it all: 'Come play with me!'

Rabbits too

Welfare organisations are very concerned about the conditions that most pet rabbits are housed in. When we consider these animals in the wild, we can appreciate that they require a lot of space to run around in. Sadly stores sell small hutches that are effectively rabbit prisons, and the poor animals soon suffer from muscle wastage and mental distress. Rabbits need access to a safe run, which should measure a minimum of fourteen feet by six feet (approximately four by two metres). A neighbour told me that he had noticed a wild rabbit visiting the area where he kept his son's pet rabbit, and peering into the tiny pen. Until then, the man had not noticed the anomaly of what he was seeing, or the grotesque injustice.

I first met Amber, a rabbit expert, many years ago during filming for the TV show *Animal Roadshow*. She has rehabilitated numerous rabbits rescued from unsuitable conditions, and can testify to their intelligence and sense of fun. As a child, she and her family had pet rabbits who were free to run around inside the house and outside in a secure garden, and she became used to their play antics. The rabbits created games of their own such as crawling under a bed, then suddenly darting out at a child's feet to make him or her jump before dashing back under. The bunnies also poached socks and items of underwear off radiators, stashing them around the house and garden. Many a morning started with a laugh-inducing hunt for clothing stolen by a rabbit!

Pet rabbits show they know the value of play through their antics

Incredibly, one day Amber witnessed a group of bunnies working together as a team. They were playing in the garden when they started to take an interest in the lane beyond, bobbing up and down by the gate, whiskers twitching inquisitively as they peeped through the slats. Amber was not unduly concerned because the gate was heavy to push open. The rabbits, however, had formulated a plan, and Amber was amazed to see the group push in unison on the gate so that it swung open. Then a few of them remained with their bodies pressed on the gate, preventing it swinging back shut so that all the rabbits in the garden could dash through into the lane beyond for a daring adventure. Amber said that witnessing the rabbits' antics was like watching a Disney movie.

Keys to being playful

- Get plenty of rest to help improve your alertness, creativity and mood. Rest is a key factor in supporting animal health and wellbeing. Remember that we humans are animals too, and problems occur when we neglect to replenish our bodies through relaxation and sleep.
- Be open to having fun instead of dismissing a light-hearted attitude as trivial.
- Play helps us develop a sense of humour.
- Laughter is good for us. Scientists believe that human laughter evolved from a distinctive panting emitted by our ape relatives during boisterous play. The panting functions as a signal that those play actions are good-natured.
- When we feel pressures from work or home circumstances, a break of even a few moments can help ease our concerns. From cats to wolves, horses to leopards, dogs to elephants, the creatures around us routinely play to relax, invent, discover, and bring amusement to their day.

Play therapy

Playing with animals benefits humans in terms of helping us evolve. During a discussion with Dr Risë VanFleet, an international expert in Animal Assisted Play Therapy™ and co-author of *Animal Assisted Play Therapy*, I discovered some interesting facts about how this works and why it is so important for us.

As with young animals, play allows children to use their creativity whilst developing dexterity and their cognitive, emotional and social skills. Play in any species is important for healthy brain development, stimulating richer neural connections. Canids, which includes wolves, jackals, foxes and domestic dogs, have a distinct code of play that incorporates boundaries and rules, clear communication signals, apologising when necessary and being straightforward. Play, as we can see, is a social necessity.

In her play therapy work with children and families, Risë includes as teachers mostly dogs and horses – however, cats, rats, goats, and birds can also have a therapeutic effect. Play is a way of communicating beyond words, so in this way Risë helps children struggling with an issue, as they can bring it out during play. These skills are the building blocks of positive human interaction and remind us to consider others – even when we are having fun. The animals that are present are invited to interact with the child to help teach the myriad lessons on offer through the act of play. We need to be mindful that animals too can express inner turmoil through play, and therefore guard against labelling chaotic or aggressive animal play as being naughty or bad. An animal can be emotionally and mentally adversely affected by factors such as weaning too early, the health of the mother, sibling rivalry and competition for food, breeder handling, home circumstances, human attitudes, training issues, lifestyle needs not being met, illness, pain and many other factors. For this reason Risë carefully selects, socialises, trains, and monitors her play therapy animal partners to ensure that they can be happy and healthy teachers.

Success with Katie

Risë has experienced for herself how, as well as being healing for us, play heals animals too. Many years ago, Risë was involved with an animal shelter that took in a traumatised puppy from a puppy mill, who quickly escaped by climbing a fence. For two months the puppy, now named Katie, lived wild in the surrounding woods until she was eventually found. Terrified of everything and everyone, including other dogs, the pup's future seemed uncertain, so Risë took Katie home. With her expert knowledge, Risë set up a programme of play sessions involving her older dog, Kirrie. Over the years Kirrie has proven herself to be a wise, patient and gentle playmate who loves to help troubled souls – human and animal.

Gradually Risë saw a shift in Katie as a playfulness began to emerge. As this progressed, social skills developed until Katie became evidently more and more comfortable with life. Through safe play Katie learnt to express herself and reveal her true personality.

Our role

During Risë's work as a play therapist, the humans present are taught to respect the animals as well as how to interpret their responses. It is important that we don't project our needs and wants onto animals when we play with them – rather it should be a mutually beneficial happy interaction. Building a fun relationship means that animals should not be restrained during play, and the animals should be able to volunteer their assistance rather than be made to do something. Through playing with animals we can learn to pay attention to how they think and feel as well as get to see their personalities. This helps us in life to build meaningful connections with others.

It's important too that animals, including pets and horses, have the freedom to choose and create recreational activities, just as we wish to. It's one of the reasons why I dislike zoos and marine parks, due to the deprivation of the fundamental rights of wild animals.

Play is an interaction

I was alarmed to read in my morning paper that a new gadget had been developed which busy people can activate using their smartphone. The gadget can be remotely triggered to roll across the floor in order to entertain an animal left on its own, and also contains a camera and a microphone. Let's stop and think about this – a lonely pet is supposed to feel comforted and loved by the sudden movement of a ball? It seems to me that the real idea is that this alleviates guilt in people who leave their cat or dog alone for long periods.

Dogs and cats can instigate games by themselves if they choose to, but more often than not they seek the presence of a playmate. Such gadgets may well have a useful role if a dog is left alone – but only on occasion. No dog should be regularly left alone for more than a few hours without being visited by a human, for example a neighbour or professional pet carer. Best practice advice from animal behaviourists is that dogs should be left by themselves for no more than four hours at a time, although a little longer might be OK for if there is more than one dog and they can act as company for each other, and they have access to an outdoor area – provided that nuisance barking is not an issue and the dogs are safe and not stressed by their surroundings.

If a dog is regularly left alone for over six hours, there should be serious concerns for the mental and emotional welfare of the animal, the treatment of which might breach welfare laws.

As responsible dog owners, we should consider whether there are any separation-related issues that would cause distress to the dog if left alone. A study at Bristol University suggests that dog anxiety due to owner absence works across a spectrum, so that dogs may not actually display distress behaviours, such as destruction or barking, but instead become depressed and withdrawn.

To me, an inanimate object is never going to provide any measure of companionship for a sentient being. Would we find it acceptable to leave a child unattended for hours with only their iPad for company and entertainment? It doesn't work that way; as the stories in this book show, play is an interaction.

> Play in the animal kingdom is also sport. It is simultaneously frolicking and serious, trivial yet meaningful. Rules and conventions underpin the games. Because nonhuman animals have been on this planet longer than we human animals, play is older than humanity and therefore part of our ancient heritage. Play doesn't separate us from our fellow animals – it unites us.

We are never too old to enjoy pastimes that we might call play. This is true of animals too; like us they need the mental and physical exercise of activity.

Animals ask that we don't just seek fun for ourselves and forget to also provide it for the animals that we look after, including cats, dogs and horses. Indoor cats become bored easily and care should be taken to enrich their environment; dogs need playtime and walking every day; horses need daily free time outside and interaction with other horses.

Sunny and the cupcake

Sunny reminded me that simple things can be huge fun. It was Christmas and we were looking after my friend's house and her dogs for the holiday period. After a festive family meal, we moved onto comfy sofas to snooze in front of the fire. The four Shetland sheepdogs stretched out too, and with carols playing in the background on the radio, it was convivially restful. I was soon nudged awake by a squeaking noise, but as I looked around the room it stopped. Then it started up again, this time a longer note and louder, before developing into a full-blown crescendo of blasts, bleeps, toots and shrieks that I knew had to be made by a dog with a squeaky toy.

Three dogs were staring into the hallway. However, Sunny, the nine-month-old puppy, was not in the room, so obviously he was the one creating the music. Sure enough, he bounded into the room, chewing on a toy to create a blast of sound, then flipping the toy into the air before grabbing it again and creating more merriment. By this time everyone in the room was laughing as we shared the happy waves of energy that Sunny was stimulating.

'What have you got there?' I asked Sunny, and he trotted over to drop a plastic cupcake in a festive design – red with a green holly shape on top – at my feet. Games started then between the humans and the dogs. Blue, the oldest dog, grabbed a bright yellow tennis ball to carry around, Connie picked up a soft toy pink octopus and dangled it from her mouth, Gina chased the toys that we tossed about the room but didn't pick up any, and Sunny carried on obliviously honking his cupcake. We all agreed later that it was the most infectious fun we had shared for a long time.

After returning home, I telephoned my friend and she had just started to fill me in on her news when a squealing noise drowned out her voice. Sunny had run into the room with his Christmas cupcake and I laughed at the silliness of it all over again.

Things that animals can teach us about the importance of play

- Pay attention to others and consider their needs.
- Behaviour has a cause and effect.
- There are rules and boundaries.
- Be fair, share and take turns.
- Consider the welfare of others.
- It helps to form relationships.

Animals bring fun into our lives in a myriad of unexpected ways; fun leads to play, something that we all need to experience – and often!

8. The Journey is Eternal

This is where I find myself. Within the secret of the Universe – the eternal core of unity.

Most of us have to deal with uncertainty about where life is taking us or cope with loss at one time or another. Our consciousness associates life with bodies, which we know deteriorate. However, events have led me and a great many other people to the conclusion that death is not necessarily as terminal as it sounds. Human and nonhuman animals have their own identity, yet are simultaneously attached to an eternal group consciousness, part of something more than themselves. My connection to animals has led me to believe that animals are aware of this group dynamic, which is why they are so attuned to their instincts and the planetary forces. Humans generally do not live their lives as if they are aware of that kind of connection, but we can do if we choose – and contact with animals as equals can help us significantly in this respect.

Infinity

I used to speculate about where my spirit would go after death. Now I know that it merges into the Oneness, as does the spirit (the life force or soul) of animals. Continuation of being is not just a privilege reserved for humans. It would seem that at the end of physical life, the life force, soul or spirit of the individual 'I' that we are – including the 'I' of all creatures – returns to a nucleus of permanence. None of us can really be sure where this is located or how it operates, although it seems to me that animals perhaps have a more natural acceptance of it as they are not bound by the constraints of any particular belief systems.

A frequent theme of animal messages is that something bigger than us exists, and we are offered tantalising glimpses into immortality and a world without spatial or linear boundaries, where time and space behave differently from how we perceive them in this dimension. This is vitally important for us to comprehend as it may help us to tackle our doubts and anxiety about what life here is all about. We are being beckoned forward to a place of greater understanding.

Shared experiences

So, what exactly happens after we've experienced this physical life and gone somewhere else? Afterlife experience is a phenomenon that has been studied scientifically. At Southampton University in the UK, the largest ever medical study into near-death and out-of-body experiences has discovered that some awareness may continue even after the brain has shut down completely. Dr David Wilde of Nottingham Trent University, involved in another study, has said, 'We just don't know what is going on. We are still very much in the dark about what happens when you die and hopefully this study will help shine a scientific lens onto that.'

Various medical doctors have come forward to discuss their thoughts about the afterlife, based on research with patients and near-death experiences. Renowned Harvard Medical School neurosurgeon Dr Eben Alexander personally experienced something so profound that it gave him a scientific reason to believe in consciousness after death. Having contracted a rare form of bacterial meningitis, Dr Alexander lay in a deep coma for several days. Even though he was bodily in a vegetative state, Dr Alexander's inner self was fully aware and in his book *Proof of Heaven* he describes exploring another, larger dimension of the Universe. What he saw and learned there convinced him that death is but a chapter in a vast, and incalculably positive, journey.

People often share stories with me about animals and the afterlife. Liz has lost count of the number of times that she has tuned into the energy of her horse Boo and sensed his presence since he passed away. One notable occasion was when Liz's cat Didi had been seriously injured and was in the veterinary clinic emergency room. A call came with the grim news that Didi's liver was failing and it very much looked like nothing could help her. During the agonising wait for an update, Liz tuned into Boo for comfort and during this connection Liz had a premonition that Didi would recover. However, Liz was very sceptical about this being a feasible outcome; so gravely ill was the cat that she dismissed the thought. Miraculously, though, Didi did start to recover but then a new problem appeared – she wasn't eating. Liz sat down and meditated to reach Boo again. Might he perhaps help Didi so that she could soon come home? Shortly afterwards, Liz was contacted by the vet who said that Didi was now eating 'like a horse'. Liz knew exactly which horse that was!

Sara mentioned a profound experience that she had after her dog Chopin passed away. Thinking of him every night before she fell asleep, Sara hoped that Chopin was at peace in his new dimension and wondered if he could give her a sign. Then, one night when Sara had stopped waiting for an answer, she had a vivid dream. Sara found herself in an arena where she used to take riding lessons. There stood a mare called Jazzberry, who had patiently taught Sara to ride horses many years earlier. By the side of Jazzberry was Chopin. Both animals stood looking intently at Sara and the realisation that they were both OK triggered a profound sense of peace in her. As relief that they were still around – albeit in a place that transcended her normal consciousness – washed over Sara, horse and dog moved away together into a bright white light. When Sara woke up she knew it hadn't been just a dream; it was the message that she had been waiting for from two friends whom she had deeply loved.

Businessman Brian had a similar experience. In Brian's dream, his much loved dog appeared. Kneeling down to stroke him, Brian found the sensation vividly real; the dog's coat was as lustrous and soft as he remembered it being during their life together. On waking, Brian knew without a doubt that the soul never dies and that knowledge dramatically changed his attitude to both his personal and business relationships.

Sometimes signs come to us in the form of everyday clues. Debbie spent the last hour of a pony's life chatting to her. If the pony would like to send a sign that all was well after she'd gone to the other side, could it be in the form of a dove, Debbie asked, so that she would understand the message. When soon after a dove landed in front of Debbie's car and then flew up in front of the windscreen before disappearing, she spent days trying to find a logical explanation why this was not a visitation from the pony. Eventually Debbie decided that the pony's message was to believe there is a place where beings go after leaving this life.

Many varied yet comforting experiences, not just with animals but with people too, have brought me to the conclusion that there is no death – just a shift in consciousness.

Through animals, we can discover the existence of other dimensions

Teddy and the red moon

The loss of an animal companion became an extraordinary teaching. In a manner that many people will be familiar with, this particular animal had settled into my life in such a profound way that I had come to regard him as a soul mate. Extrovert, Siamese-crossbreed cat Teddy came to live with us as a ten-week-old kitten, together with his quieter, more laid-back sister Lilly. Even at that young and tender age, Teddy had an extravagant personality that offered inquisitive friendship and demanded attention. Vocal, intense and super-intelligent, he had me hooked from the first day, so that I pivoted around his commanding presence. He was not just a cat; his mannerisms and tricks made him a mix of dog, monkey and toddler too. Someone unusual was watching me through those feline eyes of deepest blue, making sure that I acted with understanding.

I loved working with the cats beside me; it helped create a peaceful foundation, enabling insights to pop into my head. When times were fraught, holding Teddy in my arms was deeply healing, especially when he pushed his head under my nose so that I breathed in his essence, oxygen for my soul.

One day, relaxing in the garden, I sensed Teddy tell me that he was not well. Turning, I saw him behind me, gazing intently. Unwavering eye contact was a feature of his interaction with humans, which in itself transmitted information about lots of things that Teddy felt were important for you to know. The sense of foreboding was numbing, although Teddy looked well enough and nothing in particular had changed as regards his behaviour. Acting on my intuition, I took him to the veterinary clinic. While I explained my concerns that something was wrong, the vet watched my cat strolling around the room, rifling through a box, opening drawers and tapping papers onto the floor. Questions were asked about the symptoms of his illness, which I had to admit were not present. I just had this horrible gut feeling that something was not as it should be. The bemused vet gave Teddy a thorough examination and, enjoying the attention, the cat purred loudly. Given a clean bill of health, Teddy and I were sent on our way. All the same, I suspected our carefree days were coming to an end.

Some months later, physical signs of illness became apparent as Teddy suddenly became very restless. Back to the vet we went and blood tests showed a thyroid problem, so medication was started. Things went downhill rapidly after that, as Teddy developed diabetes. There was something worse going on, though, because through my hands I sensed the energy of a tumour. People often ask me what I mean by that statement and I try to explain it this way. When I touch an animal I may sense either brightness like a glow under my hands, or a focal area of darkness called an energy blockage. The realisation that I was perceiving this sort of congestion did not bode well and it dawned on me that the unbearable day was close when Teddy, who had been my teacher for fourteen years, would no longer be part of our home.

A scan revealed that my premonition of a tumour was correct; by now it was large and invasive. Teddy fought to stay, trying to carry on as normal, but his strong will was not enough to combat the encroaching weakness of his ailing body. The bleak day quickly came when the vet was called to the house to help release my soul mate from suffering.

During our last precious minutes together, I wanted to stay in a mindful state so that I could give Teddy the best possible healing send-off. It would have been grossly unfair if I had been so wound up in my sorrow that I failed to offer him the help that I give to animals in a professional capacity. Although I know that all beings transition at the time of physical death to another level of consciousness, I can't be sure whether that stage is easy or not and I suppose it depends on various factors. However, in my experience healing nearly always offers peace, which helps with the transition between worlds.

Whilst murmuring to Teddy to follow the light that would appear before him, I felt a familiar blending of our souls, a beautiful reassuring sensation that overrides species separation. Whispering my thanks for the treasured honour of knowing him, I sensed Teddy's departure; a soft, brief movement of air through my fingertips like a candle flame being extinguished. Then came the brutal realisation that Teddy's physical body no longer supported life. At that point, Lilly sprang up to stretch fully alongside her brother as she had done every day since their birth. Lilly, her warm vibrant body filled with loving sentience, was conveying her own farewell message. Holding the distraught bitterness of my grief together until Lilly had done what she needed to, I watched the clock and it was a full five minutes before she moved away to sit in a favourite chair.

There is a transition at the time of death to another place and level of consciousness, of that I am certain. Something is going on which from time to time we are privileged to glimpse; I call it the place of 'Otherness'. From that dimension Teddy, I strongly believed, could continue to add to my knowledge from beyond the barriers of time and space. He would not cease to involve me in lessons just because he was no longer physically with me.

Information about the unusual phenomenon of a super moon eclipse, a blood moon, dominated the news during the evening of Teddy's passing. It was a time of powerful cosmic energy. The moon does not possess light of its own; it shines because sunlight is reflected from its surface. During a total lunar eclipse the earth moves between the sun and the moon, blocking the light supply to the moon. When this happens the surface of the moon takes on a reddish glow instead of going completely dark. The sky was predicted to be clear that night where I live and some friends asked if I would like to join them for an eclipse viewing, but I had no appetite for socialising and wanted to go to bed early. Exhausted and emotionally depleted, I gathered the duvet under my arm as I drifted into sleep and pretended that Teddy lay there beside me.

I woke with a start and, grabbing my watch, noticed it was just after three o'clock in the morning. Feeling as though driven by an important instruction, I had a compelling urge to go outside into the garden. After pulling on my clothes, I wandered down the path until I came to a place near to an old apple tree which offered me a clear view of the moon. It truly was spectacular due to the extraordinary surreal illumination. More than that, though, was a sensation of intense sparkly atmospheric energy, which caused me momentarily to tremble.

Most noticeable was the overwhelming sensation that Teddy was with me – and simultaneously it dawned on me, in a flash of deep insight, that he was everywhere and in everything. He was in the light of the moon, the strength of the trees and the solidity of the ground that I stood on. He was the owl hooting in the distance and the rabbit hopping through the grass. Turning this way and that, I noticed that, seemingly superimposed in the structure of all that I surveyed, was a cat. Teddy was all around me and within me and at the same time, incredibly, I knew that I also stood in the midst of that energy of everything. It came as a further shock to sense that we are *always* everywhere, including the repercussions from our past actions and thoughts. It was a wake-up call to try harder in my quest for mindfulness, as well as a confirmation of our oneness. Theoretical physicists believe there are an infinite number of universes with different variations of beings, and situations, taking place simultaneously. I have long thought this to be so, and Teddy was sealing that knowledge within me.

I was being reminded too that the moon that I looked at that night was above each of us, part of the same Universe that we all belong to. I was there and Teddy was there, as was everyone and everything, revealing that all life forms are everywhere all of the time. The condition which we call death does not diminish that energy process. For the first time in my life I fully understood the phrase 'everything is connected' – a mantra which has been the foundation of spiritual teaching for many thousands of years. Experiencing the connection for myself in this way, it was no longer just a concept but a reality. Implied too was that the overarching problem with the human condition is our separation from this awareness. Because the repercussions of our thoughts and actions reverberate everywhere, our eternal legacy lies in what we do and how we nurture relationships with all beings when in a physical form.

The atmospheric energy that night was so strong that I felt its hum synchronising with the flow of each individual life, past and present. My breathing quickened with a similar resonance and I understood that Teddy was now revealing the existence of the combined pulsating breath of all life, as well as its everlasting continuation and development. We don't cease to be, we can only shift dimension. As soul beings, our lives are invincible.

Being a harvest full moon, this blood moon was also said to be an indicator of change and new beginnings. When the moon is closest to Earth due to its rotation and orbit, this is a time when the energetic effects of the moon are felt the most strongly – which proved to be the case for me. As I turned back to the house it felt like incandescent streamers of light were flowing with me, so strong was that magnetic moonlight. As I lay down in my bed again I was aware of Teddy's presence alongside my body. It was more than just a vague, hopeful sense of him being there, I *knew* he was beside me.

Peaceful sleep enveloped me, replacing the anguish of loss. The whole of the next day, I relived that extraordinary and profound nocturnal journey into the other-worldly territory, which had nevertheless been strangely familiar to me. It was a time to remember that the mysterious power at the heart of creation sparkles in all beings. We are invited to honour this knowledge, instead of besmirching magnificent experiences with petty pessimism and negative thoughts caused through doubting our sensitivity. When we accept the revelation of a mystery, then in my experience there will be other such occasions on offer. The events may be incomprehensible and unexplainable but they are fabulous experiences all the same. This is what I scribbled down the morning after the red moon as I responded to Teddy's voice in my heart:

> *The flow of life has no agenda or timescale, it simply is. The soul unfolds through life as required, and because it is a timeless state it is not hindered by today or tomorrow. The soul concerns itself with spiritual growth and movement. This is why being aware of the lesson in each moment is the ultimate state of listening, an awareness of actions and interactions and how it affects the whole. Life moves forward at its own pace, and to receive inspiration we need to absorb the resonance of animal voices.*

A few days later I stood by a horse and heard thousands of animal voices say:

> *Measure your life less. Listen more. Give love to all creatures equally. Take something from me, leave something with me. In equal measure. Because I am you and you are me.*

The aching hole that had opened within me after Teddy's death was healing, leaving gratitude for the time that I share with animals in its place. When I discussed the teachings I'd learnt from my years spent with Teddy with an Australian friend, she quoted this Aboriginal proverb: 'We are all visitors to this time, this place. We are just passing through. Our purpose here is to learn, to grow, to love. And then we return home.' Yes indeed, wise words from an ancient culture.

When an animal passes away, if we have other animals in our care we must devote time and attention to those companions, realising that they too will feel a sense of loss and shock, and need our help to recover. The dynamic in our relationship with them will change too and we can get to know them in a new way as they will have things to teach us that are relevant to the time. Sometimes I hear people say that they will never have another animal companion because they don't want to go through the distress of grief again. I can understand those sentiments, but for my part the experience and learning, not to mention the love shared, far outweighs the trauma of parting – and a life without animal friends is too empty for me to contemplate.

Soon after Teddy departed, Emma got in touch. She was filled with sadness, having said goodbye to her old horse, Pru, and she wrote: 'If

I can't hold the vastness of the grief, I can't hold the vastness of the love we shared' – a beautiful sentiment. Emma was indebted to Pru, who over the years had taught her that each individual animal is worth getting to know for their invaluable teaching. On contacting the sanctuary where Pru had come from, Emma found two more horses who needed a home. The mutual benefit of friendship, caring and learning continues.

The old dog

Mia was sixteen, deaf, with poor eyesight and legs wobbly with arthritis, but she was still sharp mentally. Among a pack of five dogs, she was the wisest owing to her age and experience. It was impossible to ignore her voice; I didn't need to be facing her to hear her messages, so strong was her energy despite her physical weaknesses. Yet at the same time there was a delicate feminine aura about her, and her inner strength was gentle.

I was looking after the dogs while their owners were away on holiday. By now, Mia was struggling to walk so her people had asked me to leave her at home when I took the other, younger dogs down to the beach. Mia watched me with disapproving eyes and her sadness overwhelmed me. The next day, when I told her she was coming to the beach too, she trembled with anticipation. As my feet touched the sand and the dogs started sniffing at the rocks, Mia came over and stopped right in front of me, almost touching me with her nose; then she performed a small bouncy jump as high as her legs allowed her to, all the time staring up into my eyes. I sensed her voice telling me that she knew she did not have long left on Earth, and that living life to the full was what she yearned to do. There was no point in holding back on fun. 'Thank you for bringing me to the beach,' she whispered into my mind, and then she wandered off, her poor sight and deafness leaving her oblivious to my calls when she strayed too far from the group. I got some much needed exercise running after her, and she had a lot of fun that day and during the days that followed. Mia passed away in her sleep a few weeks later.

After a few months I revisited that part of the beach and stopped to poke about in the rock pools. Something brushed against my leg but when I turned to look, I could see nothing. Then, in my mind's eye, I saw Mia and felt her with me, her presence as dominant as if she were there in physical form. Everything that she had experienced in this life Mia had retained for eternity, including her happiness and joy at the beach. It reminded me of our responsibility to animals, to give them a good, full life. What we do matters not just to the animal but to us, for it shapes who we become. It is our legacy for when we too transition from this place. We are eternal souls too.

All of life

From time to time I come across injured wildlife and the depth of life-force energy in these creatures always amazes me. You can feel it humming in your hands, a vibrant will to fulfil the complete circle of birth, maturity and then the journey beyond this physical life. No matter what creature I am with, the only difference between them and me is spoken language, otherwise we are all of equal worth. There is a richness of experience in even the humblest creature, which longs to impart to us its legacy of knowledge and experience. Holding a bird, a tiny rodent or a baby animal, I have come to understand that size does not indicate anything other than that some animals are big and others are smaller. The emotions, thoughts and feelings in a tiny animal, for example, can be sensed with the same volume of energy as those of an elephant. Grief is something that in my experience all animals experience when a friend or family member – human or nonhuman – departs. All animals have interior lives in this respect. Under the skin they are connected to us like kin, they are not aliens. Animals are waiting patiently to offer an important corrective to our human species' misguided sense of exceptionalism, and fortunately science is now catching up with what has long been obvious to those who live with animals.

Consciousness, empathy, emotions, altruism and communication are not exclusive to humanity, and I wonder why it has taken science so long to acknowledge the truth about the nature of animals. Perhaps the delay has been because the burden of responsibility is daunting and it would mean a complete change in terms of how we view animal welfare? Humanity has yet to take a further step collectively, and accept that the life force of an individual – their energy signature – seems to continue after it has left the physical body. This too has immense implications and opens up a wide new avenue of potential discovery and learning. Teddy guided me a little way down that mysterious pathway and a great many people around the world have had similar experiences for themselves. There is so much more that will be revealed, I am sure, as scientists increasingly research our experiences of the world; and the experiences of animals should be included in those discoveries too.

The vision

Life has many ups and downs, and can be quite harrowing at times. Most of us probably wonder at some point, 'What is my life's true purpose?' When we are caught up in doubt, our motivation can become dampened and we might feel overwhelmed and discontented with our lot.

At the bottom of a hill in rural England, there is a place where many years earlier the existence of the 'Otherness' confirmed by Teddy was revealed to me by a dog. At the time, I had volunteered to take my neighbour's dog, Cassie, out for walks, and for several weeks she had been my solace. A favourite route of ours took us first into a meadow, then, after passing through a gate, we would wander down the hill to a disused quarry, where Cassie loved to splash in a pool. By the gate was a large moss-covered rock, presumably originating from the quarry, where I liked to stop and think. Whenever I did this, Cassie would usually bound about around me in the long grass, sniffing the undergrowth.

On this particular day, I was feeling as if I had lost my way through life and I sat by the rock feeling completely drained. 'Is there a point to being here?' I shouted out to whoever might be listening. 'If there is, please show me.' Cassie appeared and licked my face before turning to sit with her back leaning against me. Wrapping my arms around Cassie's body, I buried my face into her fur, submerging myself in her comforting presence.

Something weird happened next. It seemed at the time like I fell asleep but I can't have done, not whilst crouching down hugging a dog. In a split second, I found myself transported into a dimension beyond my normal level of consciousness. I was somewhere else, neither higher nor lower than this world, just different. I vividly remember staring at what looked like pillars of smoke and briefly thinking that the meadow was on fire, yet I was strangely powerless to move out of the way. The columns, though, were soundlessly moving from side to side – and then I realised that they were not artefacts but opaque, ethereal beings of light with human form.

Then the shapes swirled around and through their shifting turned into animals of all species. A lion, sheep, buffalo, an elephant, horses, cats, giraffes, fish, whales and dolphins – countless species formed as I watched the spectacle unfold. Birds also flew around in the swirling mist before me. The scene evolved again and the animals morphed back into human shapes. As this happened, the meaning of the vision dawned on me. We are all from the same source, human and nonhuman. In this place of otherness, all souls have equal significance, which means we have no right to dominion over animals, having assumed erroneously that we are the master species. It is a sobering thought, and one of the reasons that I strive to respect animals as nonhuman persons.

There *is* value and importance to our lives, even if our way is sometimes difficult. Our journey is an endless continuum. Cassie was somehow able to open a portal to show me the answer to my question, and a whole lot more. The vision ended as quickly as it had appeared, leaving me to thank Cassie for her invaluable help as well as for its selfless beauty. In losing myself hugging a dog, I had simultaneously found myself. Mindfully speaking, it was a phenomenal event. Making a pledge there and then to make a habit of listening to the voice of animals was the least that I could do – and the best decision that I have ever made. Life is eternal and so are its lessons.

9. Be a Truth Seeker

No one can be anything other than the essence of truth emerging from their being. Truth is not static, but expands or diminishes depending on our willingness to acknowledge it and act on its guidance.

Through attentiveness to the multitude of life-forms around us, we embark on a sacred adventure to discover soul truth. This adventure reminds us that truth is close by and thus relieves us of the mistaken belief that we need to seek it far away. Moreover, we carry within us the truth of who we are, because everything we have done, thought or said remains in our soul system. Many years ago, this revelation came to me through encounters with pets, horses and wildlife, and stimulated me to evolve mindfully.

Our path may seem invisible, but it is clearly visible to the Universe and, I believe, to animals, because they see our truth clearly. They don't hold back in expressing who we are, even if we can't always hear them because we are blocking guidance from our intuition. By exploring our awareness, we can arrive at a place where our path merges with that of other sentient beings. Through compassionately and altruistically tuning into all life forms, it is my experience that we can become reacquainted with our humane self – which is a manifestation of truth revealing itself.

We are constantly reminded of the need to be truth seekers, because truth does not come looking for us, although it lies all around us. Once we aspire to become such an enquirer, the Universe acknowledges our quest,

Keep searching for your truth

and amazing events appear for us to explore. Tools of spiritual knowledge can be assembled through our experiences, insights and listening to our conscience, which we can use to help us on our way.

Animals operate instinctively from this place of truth; they don't have a distorted view of life or preach false ideologies to each other – nor to us for that matter, although we don't always see it that way. There are those who might ask how I know this to be so. Simply through crossing the divide between species and blending for a while in a mutual dimension; many thousands of people the world over have similar experiences in connecting with animals in this way.

The search for truth

Time spent with animals has allowed me to glimpse realities other than the one that we normally focus on, and yet I embarked on my path almost by accident. Things kept happening that were 'weird' or 'unusual' until one day it dawned on me that I was exploring an ever-evolving chronicle. Each of our lives is a story that becomes imprinted in the Universe, but it is easy to allow the noise, opinions and caveats of others to drown out our personal voice and the voices of animals. Therefore it is crucial that we regularly take time to reflect on the story that we tell about ourselves, because this will help us to step away from negative influences and destructive attitudes.

Some may think that animals have only simplistic thoughts, but it is just that they don't have a need for complicated analysis or rhetoric. When we bother to dig deep, we find that they do possess an architecture of coherent thought and innate logic that is in harmony with the greater environment. Not only this, but they signal to us humans that we are urgently required to become passionate and careful stewards of all aspects of our planet.

Through the scope of their experiences, animals deal with intricate and subtle truths. Investigating how they do so can help us, in turn, make better sense of the events and consequences in our own lives. The quality of our lives and our relationships is reflected by the world we cohabit. We may place a lot of importance on the place we call home, for instance

– our personal sanctuary, but if we do not live mindfully, in a way that encompasses the wellbeing and habitats of all creatures, we are not living in a way that holds true to our own core values. We are behaving hypocritically.

As I have become increasingly attuned to the natural world, it has taught me that whenever I find myself in a challenging situation, something usually happens connected to an animal, either domestic or wild, that appears like a spiritual signpost and catalyst for action. If we wish to open ourselves up to these sorts of signs, we can send out a message to the source of healing that we might call 'the Oneness', or whatever name suits our way of thinking, indicating that we are open to receiving guidance. This triggers the interconnected workings of our sensitivity and consciousness on a higher level, which we can then tap into. We will be rewarded by glimpsing enigmatic truths as they flash across the radar screen of our mind. This is the process that I call 'truth seeking'. Through it, we add more new pieces to the jigsaw puzzle of our life. I would even go so far as to say that the quest for truth is our reason for being here. Some of the greatest lessons, moments of truth, are often those that we stumble across unexpectedly.

Momo

Opening my emails, I read a plea for help from an animal sanctuary in Borneo. Momo, an orangutan aged around eleven years old, had been ill for several months and was now refusing to eat. The vets were very concerned about what they could do to help him recover. Momo had been poached from the forest through the chaos caused by deforestation. Once their tree habitat has gone, apes either starve or are captured for the illegal wildlife trade, as had happened in Momo's situation.

In Malaysia and Indonesia, palm oil production has devastated vast areas of rainforest and left indigenous peoples displaced and impoverished, as well as decimating wildlife. This crop and its by-products are depleting forests required for the health of the planet, its biodiversity, and the animals, birds, insects that live within these forest habitats. Palm-oil growers have now turned their attention to the rainforests of Central Africa, where more than a half a million hectares of forest are threatened. Worldwide production of palm oil is expected to double by 2050, although there are plenty of healthier alternatives that we can choose to help our environment.

Forests are the lungs of our planet, so no matter where we live in the world, we need them to remain intact. Yet things are not just awry in these places. Environments in every country on Earth – including land, sea and air – are relentlessly being demolished and contaminated by humans, either wilfully, through ignorance, neglect, ego, greed – or just a lust to kill and destroy wildlife.

No one knows how old Momo had been when he was taken from the forest to be incarcerated as a pet, but eventually he was discovered and taken by forest police to the sanctuary with the intention of rehabilitation for his release back into the jungle. But years of deprivation, mistreatment and confinement had taken their toll, and Momo had various health and behavioural problems. Latterly Momo had developed a bacterial infection, which had already caused the death of a female orangutan called Ami, his close friend. Momo was therefore now not only very ill but depressed.

The sanctuary was thousands of miles away, so it was impossible for me to visit Momo in person and I arranged for a Skype meeting to take place. (In this way, I can work with animals in locations all around the world.) As the Skype call connected, I found myself looking at a sad orangutan in a jungle veterinary hospital. It dawned on me that if Momo had been living wild as nature intended, he would not now be adrift in an alien world. Momo was lying motionless, his head on one side and turned towards me, eyes half closed. The aura of his depleted immune system was palpable, as was his overwhelming sorrow. Touching the screen, I placed my fingers over the area of Momo's head and started to channel healing energy, directing my thoughts to the orangutan. When we offer healing, it doesn't matter whether we are physically close to an animal or many miles away, as I was in this case, because we can match the energy resonance of another being through reaching out telepathically to them. Once I had explained to Momo that I could hear him and that we could share a conversation in a communal energy space, the communication bounced between us in a continually expanding transmission of messages.

Suddenly I found myself sensing the shape of an ape, like a shadow etching in Momo's mind. He was thinking of Ami and wondering where she was. Momo ached for the comforting presence of his friend and wanted to understand what had happened to her. I explained to Momo that perhaps I could facilitate a connection through the quantum-energy levels of healing energy, creating a sort of bridge that would allow Ami to draw reassuringly close in spirit form.

In my mind's eye, I saw a ball of light gathering then dissolving to reveal the image of two orangutans side by side. 'Ami is here, she has drawn close to you,' I silently communicated to Momo. This was followed by a mental picture of the two apes walking hand in hand, surrounded by a soft light. Nothing was separate any more as worlds came together and became a buoyant circle of oneness. There was a strange, yet beautiful, sense of time tucking inside itself, dovetailing dimensions with minute precision.

My camera lay on my desk and, picking it up to record a short video of Momo for discussion during my teaching work, I was stunned at what happened next. Momo's facial expression (and I could still only see his head on my screen) rapidly changed from tense to serene, and his eyes opened wider to flick from side to side, before staring into the space by the person holding the Skype phone. Those eyes were noticeably bright and moist, as though tears were forming; the muscles around his mouth twitched slightly and relaxed … and then Momo slowly smiled, an ethereal, blissful smile. It seemed to me that a transcendental experience was taking place; animals are not exempt from such phenomena. I put down my camera to better absorb the scene that I was witnessing, which I would later describe as beatific, so deeply did the intensity of it touch my heart.

The communication energy network that had formed between myself and Momo, which now included Ami, grew and shimmered. It danced about us, shape-shifted, deepened and softened, rose and fell, and then climbed ever higher into a vortex of omnipotent magical splendour and twinkling light. The only comparison I can make is with the spectacle of the aurora borealis. The difference being that the aurora borealis is a result of the collision of electrically charged particles, and I was experiencing the antithesis of that. It was a spectacular cohesion and creation – the brilliance of the energy of permanence.

Later I discussed the session with Momo's care team. They had no previous experience of energy healing with animals and were keen to know what I had been doing, because they had seen something happen that I could not, due to my restricted view. As Momo had looked about him – and one of the vets confirmed that tears had indeed trickled onto the skin beneath his eye – he had simultaneously reached out one of his hands, curling his fingers as though taking something. The people in the room looked in that direction to see what Momo was doing, but he was seemingly grabbing thin air. Now it made sense: it had been the moment when Momo took hold of Ami's hand and they walked together in the light. To my mind, it was yet more evidence that animals are aware of multiple layers of reality and existence, which they can share with us.

Something else astonishing was revealed during my conversation with the care team. Whilst Momo was seen reaching out, one of the nurses noticed a dot of light moving slowly across the orangutan's body. The nurse tried to work out what the source was, but nothing was apparent. Then the light moved forward to touch the people watching Momo, tapping one person at a time before fading from view. I took this to be evidence of a chink that had opened in the space between worlds to allow people to see a blessing in action. We had all shared in the creative truth of the energy of everything.

The next day Momo started to eat and generally show more interest in his surroundings, and the vets were very pleased with this improvement in his demeanour. Knowing how fragile he was physically, I felt that emotional and mental improvement was perhaps the best outcome possible. For several more weeks I reconnected with Momo and it was rewarding to see him eat and play, chewing his favourite fruits or piling foliage onto his head. Jaru, one of the vets, expressed an interest in energy healing to use alongside orthodox medical care, so I gave him some healing tips. Momo seemed to understand this and was noticeably calmest in the presence of this particular vet, directing Jaru's hands to wherever he wanted them placed on his body.

One morning, whilst breaking ice on the garden pond so that the birds could take a drink, I strongly sensed Momo's presence with me, and I knew that he had come to say goodbye.

'Take my love with you, dear Momo,' I whispered into the frost-speckled trees. 'You are free now to be who you truly are.'

Some hours later I was contacted with the news that Momo, cuddled by a vet and guided by forest angels and nature spirits, had gone to join Ami in heaven's jungle. Complex thoughts and feelings relating to my intense encounter with this troubled wild animal percolated within me and I took a few days off to contemplate the myriad lessons that I needed to heed and make sense of. Numerous messages came to me during my meditations, which I have called Momo's legacy and which I will share with you now.

Momo's legacy

- Listen more.
- Don't stop learning and investigating.
- Humans forget that we own only our soul; everything else is transitory.
- The human ego challenges the soul.
- Time is a precious currency which humans waste.
- Be a peace seeker.
- Animals are attracted to authenticity in humans and repelled by falsehood.
- Humans don't know as much as other animals do.
- Keep seeking the truth in everything you do.
- Open the eyes in your heart and turn on the light.

Momo

We may be able to design machines to fly us around the world, and boats to take us across the oceans, and other vehicles in which to travel around, but as a species how much do we really understand about the world that we inhabit? Until there is a global shift in our attitude towards nonhuman animals resulting in an expansion of consciousness, the secrets that we seek won't all be revealed, because we wouldn't be able to grasp their subtleties. We have a way to go, but it seems to me that animal teachers can considerably speed up the learning process.

Ego is an enemy of truth.

Accepting truth

When I observed Momo the first time that we connected, I was reminded how the eyes reflect whatever is going on within us – they literally are 'the window to the soul'. Animals accept things as they authentically present themselves, whereas we may distort the truth to suit ourselves. Thus our version of it might actually become a falsehood and an exploitation of honesty. When there is a human tendency to skew facts in this way, other beings suffer because of the myths and misunderstanding that then become manifest. Animals are not dishonest; they respond to reality rather than create fiction.

If we wish to become truth seekers, here are some principles to guide us:
- Truth seekers take their responsibility as caretakers of all life very seriously.
- Truth seekers give their attention to improving their wellbeing and that of other creatures.
- Truth seekers turn away from negative energies and instead cultivate positive relationships.
- Truth seekers question the provenance of what they eat, knowing that the energy of distress, grief, pain and trauma of factory-farmed animals can be ingested into our system. Failure to be vigilant about our lifestyle choices and ignorance about how the products we use impact on the whole mean that we can drift into being co-creators of disharmony.
- Truth seekers talk to animals and listen to what they say.
- Truth seekers know that this life is a test of our willingness to progress as an eternal humane soul, choosing our path wisely.

Awareness is not something that we can truthfully claim to possess if we do not show consideration for other forms of life. I remember visiting a restaurant one balmy mid-summer evening where the windows were wide open. As the sun set, some beautiful large moths flew into the room, attracted by the lighting, and so I naturally jumped up to catch them and set them free outside. I was appalled at just how many diners swatted away these magnificent harmless creatures, sending them flapping onto the floor, or watched them desperately flailing against curtains as the moths tried to return to freedom.

We seek protection, yet we too need to be protectors of all life forms. A simple yet effective way to become aware of the needs of other species is to be caretakers of their needs and rights. Setting free is symbolic of letting go and releasing burdens, enabling a sense of relief to pervade our mind.

Reaching out

- Sit comfortably in a quiet place, breathing deeply and evenly.
- Imagine your heart has wings, and sense those wings gently opening to lift your heart so that your energy feels lighter.
- As you register this sensation, notice how a gentle warmth grows within you and radiates outwards. Simultaneously, a blessing of light flows into you, illuminating your senses.
- Be aware of how the energies blend and mingle, forming a mutual radiance. You are awakening to the power of your brilliance and the invitation to absorb Universal Truth.
- Allow the sensations to flow, and later write down the wisdom imparted during this experience and what improvements you wish to make to help your connection to the life around you.

Become a generous soul

We are urgently required to reevaluate our relationship with animals, and to treat all creatures with empathy and altruism. Not only does a shared sense of morality form a coherent society, but an attractive energy radiates from us when we behave morally towards other beings.

We can all cultivate a generosity of spirit through sharing what we know in order to help others. Animals are not secretive about their knowledge; indeed, they frequently draw our attention to the fact that species harmony and balance of the eco system depend on our collective wisdom.

The glory and beauty of the natural world, of which our animal companions are a vital part, embody the balance and fulfilment that we seek – body, mind and soul. We can only genuinely find this when we embrace the protection of all life.

Share your voice

Human voices are vital for telling the true stories of animals in order to ensure they receive the recognition they deserve as communicators, companions, guides, healers and nonhuman persons.

What lessons from animals in your life do you remember the most? Perhaps there is something that especially resonated with you as an irrefutable truth?

Think back to incidents when an event occurred that was extraordinary or special.
Recall the atmosphere at that time and how you felt empowered.
Encourage animal storytelling amongst friends and family. By keeping stories alive, we not only breathe life into an ancient tradition but help others to come forward and feel safe about sharing how they feel regarding animal teachings.

There's you and millions of other voices. And billions of animals talking. What we do matters, especially that we listen to every scrap of information both seen and unseen, every breath, sigh, song, bark, meow and whinny: there is truth in every voice no matter how softly whispered.

Our
path
through
life diverges
onto one track
as animals lead
us to a route we
would otherwise
not travel. The sun
shines, the wind may
blow, rain may appear.
There is light ahead and
we understand the wisdom
in the world. Our animal
guides share their secrets
and insights. On the horizon
lies the end of the road yet
also a new beginning. We
remember our purpose and
that what we do matters for
now and always. We discover
who we are as the animals
accompany us all the way home.
Healing peace fills us with Love.

Our pathway through life, when shared with animal companions, converges into one reality. It becomes a route we would not otherwise travel. We can better understand the logic of our life when animal guides share with us the secrets of their wisdom

10. Tune into Healing Energy

> 'Our task must be to free ourselves ...by widening our circle of compassion to embrace all living creatures and the whole of nature and its beauty.'
>
> Albert Einstein

I have found that the best way to widen the circle of compassion is to follow a healing lifestyle, and, as Albert Einstein advises, this means embracing all creatures and nature. There is always a strong spiritual and creative element in my work, and as you might have guessed, I am fascinated by the metaphysical element that exists in our relationship with animals, the planet and the Universe. As the animal insights and stories in this book make very clear, animals are not only our spiritual teachers, but our healers too. The stories show how we can enhance our own spiritual awareness through the use of healing energy, something that animals encourage us to do. The animals would then have completed their teaching role. Animals naturally understand healing energy, what it does and how it works, because it involves a soul-to-soul connection. Of the multitude of healing lessons that animals offer to help us flourish as human beings, they also remind us that if everyone were a healer, there would be no need for healing.

Healing is about transformation. Transformation is an interactive process for us humans, which can involve meditation, spiritual practices, interacting with animals and the natural world. Because healing energy operates on the same wavelength as intuitive communication, practising healing raises our energy vibration to the resonance of animals. In this way, our intuitive communication with them is enhanced. We can tune into an animal's signature energy through making a healing connection. This has the benefit of opening us up to better hear and understand the life-healing lessons from animals – and there are of course a great many more than I cover in this book. There are teachings that animals will bring especially to you as a unique human being, which will be relevant to whatever is going on in your life at a particular time. To be energetically primed to hear such messages is a good thing, otherwise we may miss something important.

If everyone were a healer there would be no need for healing

The healer's role

The healer, as well as hearing the message of animals, is an observer of the magnificent benevolence of an all-encompassing love. Healers are thought to act as a conduit for beneficial energy coming from a Universal Source (and we each have our own idea of what that is), which flows between the healer and the recipient, the benefits of which can be felt on many levels. Healing energy works throughout the whole being, not just in one specific area.

It doesn't matter what form of healing therapy we practise – spiritual healing or reiki, for example – healing is a mindful, life-enhancing approach. When we channel healing energy, the lessons that animals offer us come together. Healing creates a platform for learning and self-development, and healing energy is the very foundation for being able to sense and hear what animals are communicating to us. It bears repeating that healing operates on the same level as intuitive communication.

Healing and the communication link

Healing energy and intuitive/telepathic communication work on the same wavelength. Therefore, when we tune into healing energy, we open a portal for hearing what animals say and for sending messages back to them. Time and again animals display evidence of this taking place. For instance, during my teaching work I frequently get to a certain point in a presentation and a loud 'woof!' is heard as a dog sits up attentively, staring across at me from the audience, as if in agreement. This is always a cue for members of the audience to call out: 'He/she is listening to you as if they understand.' Yes, of course they do!

Often the dog wags his or her tail, looking pleased that they are participating in our learning, and sometimes a dog will even rush up to me in great excitement at being the master teacher in the room. On other occasions, it's been known for the dog to emit an audible sigh before slumping back down onto their blanket. Teaching humans, they infer, is hard work! Animals must often be mystified by humans because of our complexity and lack of awareness. Through making a healing connection we can greatly improve our interspecies understanding.

Animals as healers

The animals that we share our life with can play a role as our healers, intuitively sensing when we need comforting, and as spiritual beings they can on occasions tap into the healing source and direct it to us. Horses it seems have a particular aptitude, and not only do they respond to healing energy but they also possess a special value as healers themselves. Not surprisingly, therefore, it was horses that helped when my husband was diagnosed with a serious illness. During the difficult months before surgery I was channelling healing energy to my husband and one day he became particularly emotional, saying, 'Bella is here.' Peter described Bella appearing in his mind's eye, standing before him and transferring an insight that he should seek the help of healing horses. This came with an overwhelming sense that Peter would be OK. The image of Bella then dissolved, leaving Peter feeling suffused with her love. I knew who Bella was: a large, coloured Shire horse whom Peter had met in Canada some years earlier. At that time Bella had been living with a herd of horses who were part of a therapy programme helping heal women with life difficulties. Despite being wary of horses, Peter had bonded with Bella, and the pair would spend long periods standing close together, a silent conversation flowing between them. Since then Bella had passed away, but somehow she was aware of Peter's great need, and had appeared to transmit the important message.

It was at Mane Chance Sanctuary that we arrived a few days later, an organisation that I hugely respect for not only their pioneering work with horses as healers, but their unique and exemplary horse care. The horses live in free-roaming herds and choose how to interact with the humans, and whether they even want to. Founder Jenny Seagrove guided Peter towards a group of horses, and he stood with them for a while, but none of them were interested in his presence. Jenny took Peter to a different group and again no horse stepped forward to greet him. Peter was now rather despondent and wondering if perhaps his low emotional state was making the horses keep their distance.

We were thinking of calling it a day, but Jenny took us to another area and after a while one of the mares, Lucy, abruptly raised her head to look directly at Peter. It was as if she had heard a directive to start work. Peter then reached out to touch Lucy and she nuzzled him. Later he would describe how in that profound moment healing energy began to flow into him as a sense of deep calming peace. The energy flow increased and sort of exploded in Peter's chest area like a *thump*, causing him to stagger and bend forward to catch his breath. Lucy, satisfied with her healing work, ambled away to eat meadow herbs.

Going into the operating theatre a few weeks later, Peter imagined Bella and Lucy with him, their healing power supporting him. It produced a calming and comforting sensation.

Healing horse Lucy in action

Horses need help

There persists in the horse world great injustice towards these animals who have been a great help for humans throughout history and continue to give us great pleasure. As can be seen from the story about Lucy, horses have the ability in the right circumstances to be powerful healers. Lucy is fortunate to live in a perfect horse environment. However, elsewhere horses are still locked inside for many hours a day, and may be isolated from other horses if they are allowed outside. They also often suffer from undiagnosed pain and work that is unsuitable for them. Horses are prey animals whose natural state is to move slowly during their day to conserve energy. Humans have in many cases disrupted their world, causing horses distress on a multitude of levels. Some humans can be attracted to horses with a perverse attitude that perhaps makes them feel good because they can bully something bigger than themselves. We all have the ability to be healers, and a healer knows that it is important to treat other beings as we wish to be treated, to metaphorically hold, in our hands and heart, the soul. When we stand before a horse with humility then it releases us from the tendency to self-obsession, which can, through spiritual blindness, unleash mean-spirited and cruel actions.

The truth of a soul-to-soul connection is much overlooked in the horse world. Here's something to consider – the only thing that we own is our soul. When we depart from Earth, we leave everything behind, including whips, spurs, ropes, halters, saddles, training aids, and we face horses without any tools, only the measure of our level of consciousness. Truth is then laid bare, with no more hiding places or room for denial, and the ego finds itself dwindling. We are alone with who we are, what we became, and horses face us as the equals that they always were. It is then too late to say *sorry*.

Whilst we are here on Earth we can change what we are doing. We can strengthen the soul's desire for peace, equality, empathy and truth. The soul shuns hurting, domination and selfishness, whilst the ego seeks it. The soul, when listened to, opens our eyes to the beauty of animal wisdom and how we should treat them for our mutual benefit. All forms of life urge us to listen to their voices so that we can uncover the beauty of our soul amongst the darkness and dross that the ego conjures up and spins into a false reality. The relationship that we can then have with animals is magical and inspirational because we become, like them, beings of healing light. There is no more need to apologise, because our existence then honours life on Earth.

A message from Lucy, the healing horse

- Spend time with us in nature, because all of it existed long before humans and will probably outlast you all. Be mindful of the long history of species and how they play a role in a healing world. Once something becomes extinct, you also become diminished.
- A little humility in the face of animals releases you from the tendency to self-obsess. Then you can hear animal voices.
- Whilst animals teach you about living in the now, they also want you to learn the importance of acknowledging mistakes, your personal past, and reflecting on them so that you can act properly towards others now and in the future. In this way you gain insights into how your life intertwines with others, both animal and human, so that you can act with understanding and compassion.
- Healing horses can help you in many ways.

How to use healing therapy

Healing can be given anywhere, any time, and offers a sense of peace. It can be helpful to use healing as a preventative measure, not just when problems surface. However, during times of illness or emotional need, healing can be given every few hours. Sending healing energy from a distance through the airwaves is a very effective way of helping an animal that you are unable to be with in person.

As well as helping to restore balance on whatever level is possible, as I have suggested, healing helps improve the bond between us and animals. The truth of this was brought home to me one day when I was working with Millie, a beautiful Appaloosa mare, and her owner, Lauren, a high-flying businesswoman. The atmosphere between them was obviously strained, as Millie displayed anxiety signs in Lauren's presence, baring her teeth, flattening her ears and shaking. However, Lauren had never harmed her horse and the horse's behaviour frustrated her.

The problem, I quickly realised, was simply that the woman was so stressed, she radiated the antithesis to healing: her energy was discordant and, for a sensitive horse, like listening to shrieking noises. Turning my attention to Lauren, I gave her tips for clearing the mind, relaxing the body and using calming breathing techniques. Then I helped Lauren connect with the Source of healing energy as she stepped towards Millie. This time Millie stood perfectly still, her eyes closing peacefully. Healing energy flowed between them, and it became such a deep connection that Millie turned and wrapped her head around Lauren's shoulders.

Lauren was emotionally overwhelmed at this unusual display of affection from her horse. It was obvious from her demeanour and body language that something had shifted within Lauren's psyche at that moment which would help her not only with her equestrian hobby, but with life in general. I hold a beautiful image in my mind of Lauren and Millie standing side by side, heads almost touching, the eyes of both woman and horse looking at me, soft and shining.

Another powerful memory concerns working with a man and his dogs. After the loss of his job, Danny understandably felt very low. He worried not only about paying the bills and supporting his young family, but his self-esteem had plummeted to the point where he felt worthless. The thing that kept him going was the distracting, accepting company of his two dogs, Casper and Jammy, and long walks with them helped clear Danny's mind.

We met at a healing event that Danny was attending because he hoped it might offer him some direction in life. Like many of the people I come in contact with, Danny was convinced that he couldn't be a healer: he was not well educated, had been a bit of a jack-the-lad as a teenager, and was not religious. I explained that none of those things mattered. Animals hold out a lifeline in that they show us it is who you choose to be *now* that facilitates the switching on of healing. We are all born with healing potential and when we acknowledge it within us then we can develop and learn from its power with the guidance of our animal friends.

Danny went home that day full of enthusiasm about practising healing. Months later he sent me a message: not only was he training in healing, he had found work in a different type of company, which suited him better. 'I thought I was close to my dogs, but practising healing with them has taken my animal understanding to another level that I can't really explain,' wrote Danny. 'I am closer to my family and loving the new job because I take the healing philosophy to work with me and it helps me feel amenable and compassionate.' No doubt Danny's colleagues will benefit from his healing attitude too – and it shows how we can all make a difference. A perfect solution to the world's problems would be for everyone everywhere to act from a healing energy stance; our animal teachers would surely endorse that!

Preparing for healing

For healing to be effective we need to prepare ourselves on an energetic level.

This includes:

- Calming the mind through regular meditation, relaxation techniques and deep breathing exercises.
- Respecting and nurturing our body, including paying attention to our diet. Body energy rises or lowers according to what we eat and drink. Certain foods and drinks can over-stimulate the body or cause sluggishness, whilst other things we ingest are found to have a beneficial effect on cells. (Keeping abreast of what helps improve our health and wellbeing is something I like to do for myself, and I don't eat animal products for a variety of ethical reasons.)
- Spending time in a garden or in nature.
- Regular gentle exercise to boost our energy field.
- Listening to relaxing and soothing music.
- Restricting time spent using phones, tablets etc. Instead, enjoy creative and artistic pursuits.

The healing hand connects to a source of beneficial energy

145

What to do

- Choose a time when you will not be interrupted. Switch off distractions such as phones, TV, radios, tablets, etc.
- To create a suitable ambience you may wish to play relaxing music, such as my CDs *Animal Healing* or *Music for Pets*.
- Take a few moments to relax and calm your breathing so that you can access your inner stillness. Healing energy comes from a Universal Source and it does not matter where, or what, we think that is. As you feel a sense of calm within you, talk to the animal and tell him or her where you are going to touch them.
- Imagine a beautiful soft light coming from the healing Source and touching the top of your head, then travelling down your arms and radiating from your hands. Direct that healing light towards your animal, sending love as you do so.
- The use of healing energy is a 'doing with' process – not a 'doing to' treatment. Light, gentle touch, or holding the hand above the recipient's body, accompanied by loving thoughts and the sense that you are connecting to the Source, is what activates the flow of healing energy. You can use a whole hand or a finger/fingers depending on the size of the animal you are working with. Keep your hand still during healing therapy. The only movement should be when you carefully move your hand to a different position on the animal's body. Touch only places that the animal is comfortable with.
- Don't give healing energy instructions or have an agenda – agendas and instructions are the result of the ego interfering. Work soul to soul, allowing the Source of healing energy to work with the innate wisdom of the animal. Keep your heart centre open, sending out love unconditionally. This is the most powerful way to be a healer.
- Healing energy can be channelled through the chakra system (centres of spiritual power situated in the body), with animals having eight major chakras whilst humans have seven. The eighth and most important major chakra in animals lies over the shoulder area. This is the healing start point. If possible, the first contact will be over the shoulder area where the most important chakra in animals is located: the Brachial Major chakra.
- You can channel a complete healing session through the Brachial Major

146

chakra. From here, the healing energy travels throughout the body to where it is needed to help on whatever level is possible at the time – mentally, emotionally and physically.

- Observe the response of the animal whilst you channel healing energy.
- You can offer healing energy therapy for as long as the animal is happy for you to connect in this way. A short burst of healing can be very effective, so if you do not have much time a few minutes is helpful, provided you do not feel rushed. If the animal moves away then assume that he or she has had enough on this occasion.
- Thank the animal for the time you spend sharing this beautiful experience, talking to the animal with a loving, soft voice.

Wherever your healing journey takes you next, I hope it brings you as much joy and fulfilment as mine has brought me, and that your relationships with animals continue to go from strength to strength. After all this time working with animals, I never cease to be amazed at the lessons that these Master Teachers have to offer us. We live on a wonderfully diverse planet, and it is such a privilege to play a part – large or small – in safeguarding it for the benefit of all living beings, with the constant companionship and guidance of our friends, the animals.

The palm of your paw

In the palm of your paw
You hold the seeds of knowledge
Pointing to a revolving circle of destiny

In the palm of your paw
You nurture my heart
And lead it to discover the secret of joy

In the palm of your paw
I lay down my love to rest
Safe within your teaching

In the palm of your paw
I discover the wise secrets
Of purpose, wisdom and understanding

Useful Information

Information is correct to the best of my knowledge at time of publication but may have changed or become out of date.

Learning about animal behaviour

- *Learning About Animals* offers regular workshops near Guildford, UK. Topics include a wide range of animals and behaviour science. www.learningaboutanimals.co.uk
- *Compass Education and Training* has courses that can be taken online, for learning in your own time. www.compass-education.co.uk
- *COAPE* is an educational centre of excellence in behaviour and nutrition and has diploma training by tutors with international reputations. www.coape.org
- *TOCES* is a leading international equine distance learning college with courses for wherever you are in the world. www.toces.net

Finding a qualified animal behaviourist

- *APBC*, Association of Pet Behaviour Counsellors, has a members list of qualified and accredited animal behaviourists in the UK. www.apbc.org.uk
- *IAABC*, International Association of Animal Behavior Consultants, has courses and events, as well as a resource for finding qualified behaviourists. www.iaabc.org

Play therapy

The International Institute for Animal Assisted Play Therapy™, www.iiaapt.org

Dr Risë VanFleet, the Playful Pooch Program, Family Enhancement and Play Therapy Center, www.risevanfleet.com

Healing training

UK

The College of Psychic Studies, London, UK offers a prestigious two-year diploma course in healing. The diploma course covers a wide range of topics including a module in animal healing.
www.collegeofpsychicstudies.co.uk

The Healing Trust offers training in spiritual healing.
www.thehealingtrust.org.uk

The Harry Edwards Healing Sanctuary holds healing sessions for humans and animals, workshops and healer training.
www.sanctuary-burrowslea.org.uk

Animal Healing and Communication workshops worldwide with Margrit Coates. www.margritcoates.com

My books *Healing for Horses* and *Hands-on Healing for Pets* cover the topic of animal healing in depth, including chakra diagrams and explanations. Likewise, *Communicating with Animals: How to tune into them intuitively* is a comprehensive guide to communicating with cats, dogs, horses and other species.

USA

Healing in America's School of Energy Medicine offers certified practitioner training in energy healing. www.healinginamerica.org

Germany

John Olford offers Healing Trust courses in spiritual healing and other spiritual courses, including meditation. He is located in Augsburg, Bavaria.
www.lotus-spirit.de

Holistic veterinary organisations

The Veterinary Institute of Integrated Medicine, www.viim.org

Acupuncture

The Association of British Veterinary Acupuncturists, www.abva.co.uk

The International Veterinary Acupuncture Society, www.ivas.org

Homeopathy and herbal medicine

The British Association of Homeopathic Veterinary Surgeons, www.bahvs.com

The British Association of Veterinary Herbalists, www.herbalvets.org.uk

For USA – The Veterinary Botanical Medicine Association, www.vbma.org

The American Holistic Veterinary Association, www.ahvma.org

Mind Body Spirit music

New World Music features the world's most exciting and contemporary music for accompanying relaxation, meditation, healing, yoga, and more. Several albums are available specifically composed for playing in the presence of animals and for animal healing, as well as a meditation CD 'Animal Communication', www.newworldmusic.com

Horses healing humans

Mane Chance Sanctuary is a UK-registered charity whose horses and ponies are all rescued. A membership scheme is open to all and numerous interesting events take place throughout the year. Interaction with the healing herd is by appointment. The centre runs a visionary programme of mindfulness with horses for young people. www.manechancesanctuary.org

Other organisations world-wide offer similar services. However, as the industry is largely unregulated, thorough checks should be made for assurance that the horses are authentically honoured for their work and are properly taken care of.

Helping wild animals

There are many organisations for people to get involved with, and if every human did something to help wild creatures, the crisis of critically endangered species could be resolved, as well as improving the health of our planet. Space restriction doesn't permit me to include a comprehensive list but these are just a few of the organisations that interest me personally.

Animals Asia – a government-registered charity based in Hong Kong devoted to the needs of wild, domesticated and endangered species throughout the Asian continent. www.animalsasia.org

Durrell Wildlife Conservation Trust – an international charity on a mission to save species from extinction. Headquartered in Jersey, in the Channel Islands, Durrell focus on the most threatened species in the most threatened places. www.durrell.org

Oceanic Society – inspiring and empowering people worldwide to take part in building a healthy future for the world's oceans. www.oceanicsociety.org

Pan Eco – a non-profit foundation actively involved in nature and species conservation and environmental education in Switzerland and Indonesia. www.paneco.ch

Save Me Trust – Caring for and protecting wildlife. Giving wild animals a voice. www.save-me.org.uk

The Born Free Foundation – an international charity working throughout the world to stop individual wild animal suffering and protect threatened species in the wild.
www.bornfree.org.uk

World Wide Fund for Nature – the world's leading independent conservation organisation, determined to ensure that people and nature can thrive together for generations to come. www.wwf.org.uk

Special
Thanks

An important aspect of writing a book is the support received from other people. I am indebted to editor Sue Lascelles who has again been a valuable advisor and mentor, and done a brilliant empathic edit of my manuscript. My appreciation also goes to copy editor Helen Pisano for her invaluable help. It has been a pleasure working with the professional, helpful and dedicated team at Troubador Publishing Ltd.

Thank you to the generous hearted people who have supplied testimonials. This book contains many photos of animals, and I am honoured to have them grace these pages with their soul beauty. I am grateful to Victoria Adams, Roberta Aiello, Christa Balk, Marianne Barcellona, Liz Mitten Ryan and Sabine Stuewer for allowing me to include some of your wonderful photos. There are numerous animal loving people that my work brings me into contact with, and who share their stories with me, and for this I am humbly grateful. My life is also enriched by the wonderful human beings that I meet through my work. There are too many to name, but you know who you are. Not least, I owe a lot to family members and friends for their patience whilst I neglected my social life in order to write the book. Your support has been much appreciated. Animals have often been by my side whilst I sit and write and their presence has been both comforting and inspiring.

To all animals – thank you for being patient and loving teachers. You are my beautiful life healing guides.

Photo Credits: Victoria Adams page 13 www.littlegreenacorn.com; Roberta Aiello pages 46, 84, 115 www.robertaaiello.nl; Christa Balk pages 28, 76, 91, 102, 126 www.focusonanimals.nl; Margrit Coates pages 38. 50, 53, 60, 81, 105, 106, 138, 141 www.margritcoates.com; Liz Mitten Ryan page 45 www.lizmittenryan.com; Sabine Stuewer page 1 www.stuewer-tierfoto.de.

Illustrations: Leaf art drawing page 138, Michelle Howald; all other illustrations by Stephen Dew